## Praise for *Witch Blood Rising*

"Beautifully written, funny, engaging, informative, helpful. Every baby witch needs this book to rise strong and bring their medicine to a world that needs all the witches it can get. What I love most about this book is the tone. It's not trying to fit into a formula of witch cosplay and convince people that witches on the internet can defy the laws of physics. Instead, Asa West reminds us of the true law of witchcraft: all life is connected and our magic can help us repair the web. Read this book, and not only will you learn your magical name and how to work the crossroads, but you'll also come away with reliable knowledge of witch gods, saints, history, and mythology. You'll learn about tarot, rituals, spells, and how to become intimate with the spirits of the land. Expect Lilith, Taliesin, the Devil, and the Fairy Queen to make an appearance in unexpected ways. Most of all, this book is a call to action: tend to the embers of witchcraft burning within you. Enchantment is the fire that can and will transform the world."

—Amanda Yates Garcia, author of *Initiated: Memoir of a Witch* and host of the *Between the Worlds* podcast

# Witch Blood Rising

# Witch Blood Rising

## AWAKEN YOUR MAGIC IN A MODERN WORLD

### ASA WEST

WEISER BOOKS

This edition first published in 2025 by Weiser Books, an imprint of
Red Wheel/Weiser, LLC

With offices at:
65 Parker Street, Suite 7
Newburyport, MA 01950
*www.redwheelweiser.com*

ISBN: 978-1-57863-870-3

Library of Congress Cataloging-in-Publication Data available upon request.

Cover design Sky Peck Design
Interior by Debby Dutton
Typeset in Adobe Jenson, Alegreya Sans, and Nillota

Printed in the United States of America
IBI

10 9 8 7 6 5 4 3 2 1

*For my daughters*

# Contents

# Introduction

## The story of my name

Eleven years ago, I sat in a castle while a druid wrote me into a myth. The castle was actually a suburban home outside of Los Angeles, with a little crenellated turret over the front door. The druid was visiting California from Wales, where he worked as a bus driver to pay the bills. The owner of the house was an aging hippie who hosted events like this one and liked to send participants home with doodads she'd bought at garage sales. We'd each paid $20 to come take part in a ceremony in which the druid would help us learn our craft names. Everything I've just told you is true.

The story the druid told us was the legend of Ceridwen's cauldron. Ceridwen, as the story goes, had a son named Morfran, who was hideously ugly. Ceridwen couldn't—or wouldn't?—give him good looks, so she decided to grant him wisdom instead. She brewed a potion in her cauldron that would grant poetic inspiration, but the potion had to be stirred constantly for a year and a day, so she gave the task to an old man named Morda and a young boy named Gwion Bach.

On the final day (the druid told us), Morda fell asleep during one of his turns at stirring. Gwion, terrified of incurring Ceridwen's wrath, grabbed the spoon from Morda's hands. But when he took it, he splashed three scalding drops of the potion onto his thumb. Without thinking, he shoved his thumb in his mouth to soothe the burn.

However, only the first three drops of Ceridwen's potion would grant wisdom. The rest was a fatal poison. That meant Gwion had stolen the wisdom that was meant for Morfran, and it didn't take long for Ceridwen to find out what had happened.

Ceridwen chased Gwion, but now that he was blessed with wisdom, he knew how to escape her—or, at least, make his capture a little harder. Gwion turned into a hare as he bolted through the forest, but Ceridwen turned into a greyhound. She was just about to catch up with him when he came upon a river, where he turned into a fish. Ceridwen, undeterred, turned into an otter. Gwion then leapt from the water and turned into a bird, but Ceridwen turned into a hawk. Finally, Gwion came upon a granary filled with corn and hid himself among it by turning into one single grain. Ceridwen turned into a ravenous hen and stuffed herself until she swallowed him.

Because of the potion's magic, Gwion wasn't digested but grew into a baby in Ceridwen's womb. Ceridwen wasn't thrilled at that development, but when she gave birth to him, she found that she couldn't bear to kill him. Instead, she threw him into the ocean and let him meet whatever fate may befall him. The baby washed up on a distant shore, where a Welsh prince named Elffin ap Gwyddno found him.

Usually, this part of the story is where Gwion Bach is renamed Taliesin and begins his life as Britain's legendary 6th-century bard.

However, the druid telling us the story paused. He told us to imagine the prince opening his mouth to speak a name. The name we heard in our minds would be our craft names.

A craft name, in witchcraft, is the name you use in ritual and magic. It's the name that points to your identity as a witch, the name that captures the essence of your spiritual devotion. It may be closely guarded, spoken aloud only by your covenmates or within the safety of your ritual space. It may be public. It may be solemn, or it may be whimsical. You may carefully choose one or have one revealed to you in ritual (sometimes by a druid in a suburban house that looks like a castle). Over the years, I had tried more than once to give myself a craft name, but nothing had ever felt right. I had no idea what to expect this time. I mainly just wanted to be in a room with other witches.

But when the druid paused in his story, giving us all time to hear our craft names in our minds' eyes, Elffin ap Gwyddno said a word. *Asa. And so it was.*

We all know the power of a name. We've heard the story of Rumpelstiltskin; many of us take on new names when we enter new phases of life. In Ursula K. Le Guin's Earthsea books, a witch or wizard can summon and control a thing, but only if they know that thing's true name. "That which gives us the power to work magic sets the limits of that power," explains the Master Namer at Roke, in *A Wizard of Earthsea*. "A wizard can control only what is near him, what he can name exactly and wholly." Want to summon a hawk? You'll need to know that hawk's true name. Is it time to come of age and step into your power? If you live in Earthsea, then you need to leave your childhood name behind.

A true name contains the deepest reality of a thing, no more and no less. A name, if it's the right name, is a lens for enlightenment.

So what did my name mean? When I heard it in my mind, it was just sounds: Ah suh. But when I looked those sounds up, I found something astonishing.

I'm half Ashkenazi Jewish and a big chunk of Finland Swede, and I found out that *Asa* is a name in both Hebrew and the Nordic languages. In Hebrew, *Asa* is a masculine name that means "healer," although the Judean king it comes from, famous for rooting out idols, is a difficult figure to wrestle with as a witch. In Nordic languages, *Asa* is a feminine name inspired by the Norse pantheon, and it roughly translates to "of the gods." One who strives to heal, one who's connected to the gods, one who's both female and male, Jewish and Nordic, with moments of clarity and moments of doubt—what a perfect fit for all the churning, sometimes paradoxical parts of me. How can anyone not see the world as enchanted and alive when we're given gifts like this one?

I wanted to write about witchcraft publicly, but I was afraid to be a public witch. Back then, even just eleven short years ago, witchcraft wasn't as widely accepted as it is now. It wasn't beyond the realm of possibility that I could be punished at my job—transferred from my work with college students at the university library or denied a promotion in favor of someone less weird. So I adopted Asa as a pen name. I added the surname West as a nod to my lifelong home of California (Los Angeles, or Tongva land, to be precise), and I began to publish essays and articles as "Asa West."

Then witchcraft gradually went mainstream, in a way that it hadn't when I first discovered it in the '90s. I don't mean the empty, Insta-grammable aesthetic of witchcraft (although that's popular, too). I mean the spiritual path, the bone-deep calling, the witch fire that simmers in your blood. With the hollowness of capitalism becoming more apparent, and the Earth groaning under the weight of climate change, people started to connect with the animist worldview of witchcraft. They started to understand what makes it such a vital and beautiful practice.

Now, in my job as a journalist, I write about witchy things under my legal name. But my creative work is a spiritual offering, so I offer it under the name that is itself an offering to my path as a witch. Offerings upon offerings upon offerings, each word an expression of my love for the enchanted world around us—and a hand held out for you to join me, if you like.

Robert Cochrane, one of the forerunners of modern traditional witchcraft, wrote that the cauldron of myth and legend "means movement, a becoming of life—ever giving birth, ever creating new inspiration. There is within the Cauldron all things and all future—fate." Just as Ceridwen's elixir of wisdom required constant stirring, so is our world made up of constant change and regeneration. The druid in a suburban home outside of Los Angeles, the Welsh bus driven by a mystic: all these seeming contradictions coexist in the Goddess's cauldron.

If the divine cauldron is a thing of paradox and evolution, then witchcraft must be, too. Witchcraft constantly evolves. It gets modernized, romanticized, rebooted, and updated, even as it's continually composted back into legend. Like an optical illusion, you can look at witchcraft from one angle, and it's a bunch of people acting funny in someone's living room. Look at it from another, and it shimmers with ancient myth and magic.

This book charts my journey through a lifetime of witchcraft, in all its guises and contradictions. Each chapter examines a different aspect of witchcraft—one drop from the cauldron, if you will—through my own experience, from tarot cards to deities to spellcasting to poison herbs. It's not a comprehensive overview of witchcraft. It's just a series of lessons that one witch has learned.

Like a witch's garden, this book is sprawling and a little unkempt. It finds witchcraft in sources as unlikely as blockbuster movies and urban sidewalks. It also finds witchcraft in the usual places, like sea caves, wild gardens, and folklore. You may look at these connections as a way of renaming things we think are familiar. If you name a thing pop culture, you get half its essence. If you name it myth, you may get the other half. Is a superhero movie pop culture, or is it a myth of demigods reenacted on film? Are things like witch blood and the Devil's mark just legends, or are they remnants of some deeper knowledge? The goddess's loom, the hallucinogenic flower, the branched timeline, the antlered girl: all these images call to the witch in their uncanniness and hidden depths, no matter where in our culture they pop up. By naming things, we tap into their power. By recognizing the sacred in the mundane, we sanctify the world around us.

After each chapter, you'll find a spell in the form of a guided visualization (also known as a trance journey). These spells tie in to the subjects I cover in the chapters preceding them, and they function on both a practical and a mythopoetic level. You can work them like a traditional trance journey: Record yourself narrating them out loud, then play the recording back as you visualize the journey with your eyes closed. Speak slowly and pause often in your recording, so that the mental images have time to form as you listen. During your journey, take note of what forms the characters, places, and symbols take for you, and write everything down afterward. Alternatively, you can read each spell like a story, let it settle into your subconscious, and then see if any parts of it show up in your dreams or real life. You may be surprised at how real an imaginary journey can become after you start keeping an eye out for it. You can work every spell in the book, or none of them. You can work them after you read each chapter, or pick a few to do after you finish. It's completely up to you.

This book is the story of how I became a witch and learned to find magic in the world around me—a world that can often feel broken beyond repair, a world where it can feel like enchantment is stamped out wherever it dares to bloom. I hope that you'll recognize parts of your story in this book, too—maybe even some parts that you didn't realize you could call witchcraft. What sacred things do you find when you embrace all the jagged pieces of your story? What power can you summon when you give those pieces new names? If this book plays some small part in your journey, then it'll have done its job.

## A Spell to Find Your Name

There's a castle somewhere close to you, but you've never seen it before. Not really. (Maybe this is a literal castle. Maybe it's purely in your mind. Maybe it's not recognizable to anyone else. What do you think?) Fill your pack with the treasures you'll need for the journey: some nourishment, an offering, and a reminder of home.

To get to the castle—to *really* get there—you'll need to take a path you've never taken before. Don't be afraid, although the path will be dangerous. Plot it out on a map. Feel your way with your senses. Conjure the way with your magic. You'll need to pass through forest and water and the high places of the air, but don't worry: There are three guides waiting to help you. Be sure to share some of your nourishment with each of them. You have plenty to share.

Find the first guide—the guide on the forest floor. They'll lend you their camouflage. Can you see how wonderfully the camouflage suits you? It fits perfectly. It looks beautiful on you, even as you seem to melt into your surroundings.

Find the second guide—the guide in the water—who will lend you their speed. How powerful you feel, zipping through the current! How easily the miles fall away!

Find the third guide—the guide in the air. Jump up to meet them, and they'll lend you their clear sight. Look how magical the world is, now that you can see its countless details. Feel your understanding of it blossom.

On your journey, you'll come to a point when you think you'll never make it to the castle. The monsters are loud here, but consider this: If they were going to get you, they probably would have done so by now. Don't lose heart. Take in some of your nourishment. Have a rest, but not for too long. Trust in your camouflage and speed and clear sight. Keep going, and you'll reach your destination.

Sure enough, the castle soon lies before you. When you get there, knock three times and the gate will open. Don't go inside until you've left your offering at the threshold.

When you're inside, a surprise awaits you: It's someone who's very familiar to you. Or maybe it's not such a surprise after all.

Who else would be waiting to give you your true name? Approach them. Can you feel how much they love you? How long they've been waiting for this moment?

When you reach them, they'll speak your name out loud. That name is—

_____

—and it's perfect. It's always been your name. You just didn't know it.

You're alone in the chamber at the heart of the castle, which is actually the deepest chamber of your own heart. Take out your reminder of home, and it will take you home.

When you're back, have a snack. Pat your body to get resituated in the mundane world. Say your name three times—the name that comes from the deepest part of you, the name that helps you remember who you are.

# 1

## The Devil's Mark

### On demons, bloodlines, and knowing you're a witch

I was born with a nickel-sized birthmark on my right arm, which left a dramatic scar when the doctor removed it. When I was a kid, my mother told me to tell people I was grazed by a bullet. I think she was joking. Partly, she liked the idea of an entertaining story. Partly, she may have been embarrassed that her offspring had come with something so grotesque.

My father once told me a funny story about the night he and my mom brought me home from the hospital. It was January, and they laid me in my cradle wearing only a diaper and then huddled under their own thick blankets against the January chill. They wondered why I wouldn't stop crying, and it took them a long time to realize that I was freezing. My mom's pregnancy had been accidental, their wedding a hasty affair in a relative's backyard a few months before my birth, and I think the last thing my parents wanted to do was spend the rest of their lives being parents. They didn't know to put a blanket on me. They hadn't asked for the hardest job on Earth. The weird birthmark must have been the icing on the cake.

In high school, after I hit a low period and took a handful of Tylenol, I came upon my dad reading my notebook of angsty poetry and crying. "I love you so much," he said. Even now, though, I force myself to believe it. How could anyone love something as monstrous as me?

What makes someone a witch? How does someone turn from an ordinary person into that uncanny creature of legend? When does that strange seed get planted? Sometimes practitioners talk about witch blood, witch fire, inherited legacies, ancestral lines. According to a letter that my great-grandmother wrote in Yiddish, her mother Esther was a *folks froi*, or "folk wife," in Poland. Women went to her for medicine and healing, and based on what we know about Jewish folk magic, it's possible that she made amulets to ward off the baby-killing Lilith. If having a witchy ancestor is a requirement for authentic witchery, then I fit the bill—along with every other human being on Earth. (After all, our collective ancestral pool is a lot smaller than we think it is.)

Other practitioners see witch blood as metaphorical, bolstered by ancestors of spirit more than ancestors of blood. The witch blood, the numinous spark that flares in your brainstem, is a calling that anyone can answer, a lightning bolt that can hit any skull. The witch blood snakes through the meridians of the Earth, flowing toward those who can perceive it, and rises through the body out of the living soil. The witch fire seeks whom it seeks, tapping those who may make good vessels. If you answer the call, you step into a life that's often as lonely and painful as it is beautiful. If you ignore that call, you may spend all the years of your life ignoring the deepest need of your soul—and still suffer the ostracization that you were hoping to escape. If you have the witch blood, you're marked, whether you embrace it or not.

In 1486, German priest Heinrich Kramer published the infamous witch-hunting manual *Malleus Maleficarum*. It aimed to stamp witchcraft out, but arguably helped fuel its modern revival, too. The *Malleus Maleficarum* is a fever dream of misogyny and paranoia, detailing witches' pacts with Satan and the best ways to torture confessions out of women. In teaching aspiring witch hunters how to identify a witch, Kramer took the idea of the witch's mark quite literally. The book instructs inquisitors to strip accused women naked and shave their bodies, because witches are "in the habit of hiding some superstitious object in their clothes or in their hair, or even in the most secret parts of their bodies which must not be named." The book explains that these objects are amulets given to the witch by the Devil. However, in practice, inquisitors decided that amulets could also be "sewn into the skin" so that any mole or blemish could be interpreted as the Devil's mark.

When I first read that passage, I thought of two things. First, Buffy Summers's birthmark in the movie *Buffy the Vampire Slayer*. Buffy's mole marks her as the fabled Slayer, destined to keep the global vampire population under control, and her guide, Merrick, is appalled when he finds out that she's had it removed. At first, reading Kramer, I fantasized about being Buffy, being chosen. Only much later did I think of my own birthmark.

Of course, that first mark will always be abstract to me, because I never actually saw it. For me, it's only ever been a scar. By the time

I was in middle school, though, another birthmark on my back had grown to the size of a quarter. A doctor removed it and found precancerous cells, so they called me back in to cut away more around the edges. In college, I had yet another mole removed, and still another in grad school. Dangerous birthmarks became one of the patterns of my life, sprouting from my skin like mushrooms after rain.

There's a mundane explanation for all my marks: It's genetic. But what would Kramer and his witch hunters have thought if they'd seen them?

Once, drifting through half sleep in the middle of the night, I saw a ball of fire arc past my bedroom window. I jumped up, jolted wide awake, and ran to the window to see if the backyard was burning. The ball had been huge, like a comet, blue, and almost pixelated. Was it ball lightning? A hypnagogic dream? I'll never know for sure, but by the time I got to the window, every trace of it was gone.

I saw other strange things growing up, too. I dreamed that I was lying in my backyard and a brown pegasus flew overhead. I gradually came to think that God looked like the *Mona Lisa*. It all feels silly now, but I grew up in a place where the only spirituality was found in Evangelical megachurches. There were no wild places near me, just endless miles of lawns and strip malls. The visions were funny, even absurd, but when I had no frame of reference for real mysticism, it felt like Divinity had to use whatever symbols I would understand.

Kids at school called me "zombie" because I spent so much time staring into space. It wasn't just the visions that distracted me—things weren't great at home, and I often stumbled late into class with my teeth unbrushed and my homework undone. I didn't have any friends. Eventually, my hair started growing in curly, and the kids had a field day with my sudden frizz. I didn't know how to be normal.

Some strains of traditional witchcraft, including a stream of witchcraft inspired by British and European folkways, incorporate the myth of the Nephilim into their origin stories. In Jewish lore, the *Nephilim* are semi-divine giants, not unlike the Titans or jotuns of Greek and Norse mythology. The Nephilim are born from human women impregnated by angels, and in some versions of the myth, those angels are the fallen followers of Lucifer. In fact, the word *Nephilim* is related to the Hebrew root for "fall." This origin story for witches is even better than having an ancestor who made amulets. According to this belief, a witch isn't just an unhappy misfit. I wasn't just an unhappy misfit. If you believe in the Nephilim, you can believe that you're guarded by something more ancient and powerful than the people who pick on you. That force, that deity, goes by countless names: Cernunnos, Pan, Bucca, Herne the Hunter, Azazel, Janicot, Puck, the Initiator, the Trickster, the Old One, Light-Bringer, the Devil—not the Satan of Christian mythology, but the initiator of magic and the keeper of primeval wisdom. The spirit and embodiment of our most feral selves, the one who calls witches to the ecstasies of the Sabbat. If you believe in witchcraft, you can believe that the Devil in all their guises recognizes your bloodline and marks your body as a signpost to your future self.

Why do we tell ourselves stories of sacred marks and other-worldly ancestral lines? Is it pure ego, or does it come from a need for acceptance? Why can't a witch simply be someone who casts spells, or worships a goddess, or dances under the moon? I suppose it's because when you feel strange and disliked, when you never seem to belong in the place where you ended up, you search for a reason why. You search for an explanation in the chaos. You search for signs that somewhere, something is taking care of you.

Witches love talking about trauma. We're compelled to talk about it because so many of us carry it. Dredging up our pasts helps us understand what exactly we've survived, transforming our pain into something useful.

Definitions of trauma sometimes include two components: inescapable shock and a sense of helplessness. A painful or frightening experience becomes traumatic when you can neither fight nor fly. The bully hits you and you have nowhere to run; a parent disappears and you're told to shrug it off. The neural pathways in your brain become frozen in a loop, trying to solve an impossible problem. How do you make your subconscious understand that the crisis is over? How do you get feelings off your chest when no one's there to listen? That first night home, when I lay freezing in my bassinet, is gone from my conscious memory but embedded in my being. The trauma of the newborn, cold and frightened and seemingly abandoned. The trauma of overwhelmed new parents, trapped in a house with the sound of their stolen futures.

When I think of trauma, I think of Lilith, written in Jewish legend as the Devil's wife, and regarded by witches as a matron goddess of magic and rebellion. We all know the origin story: she's Adam's first wife, who's exiled because she refuses to be his subordinate. One satirical Jewish text states that she flees because Adam won't let her be on top during sex. (Joke's on him—every guy I've been with loves it.) Some scholars believe she evolved from the Akkadian demon Lilitu, while others have traced her to a Mesopotamian spirit called a *lilu*. According to some legends, she marries the Devil and lives with him by the Red Sea. She's responsible for wet dreams. She kills sleeping infants in the night. She could be considered the first witch: She chooses chaos over order, freedom over subservience.

The connection between Lilith and babies isn't just a superstitious explanation for SIDS. Jungian scholar Barbara Black Koltuv writes, in *The Book of Lilith*, that "the forces of Eve, mother of all living things, and Lilith, spirit of Night and Air, are evidenced in women's conflict between giving birth and nurture to children, and needing to produce and nourish ideas and works." Koltuv explains that as a woman "attempts to meet the needs of her children, her work, and herself, [she] can suddenly feel the fiery uprush of Lilith's murderous rage." Our culture insists that women can *only* be mothers, even though we're so much more. No human being can emerge from that kind of psychic pressure unscathed.

A few years ago, my mother came out with a weird warning: She told me, out of the blue, that I'd better not ever get an abortion. That was the moment I suspected that she'd considered aborting me. Realizing something like that leads to a strange existential paradox. These days, I'm very glad to be alive, but I also wish she'd chosen her own fulfillment.

And what if she had? She could have followed Lilith, ending her pregnancy and leaving her boyfriend and continuing the wandering that took her from New York to San Francisco. Instead, she followed Eve, obeying the new life inside her and becoming a wife and mother.

One effect of trauma is a loss of access to intuition. Traumatized people can have trouble understanding what their instincts are telling them. You don't know how to process the feeling of wrongness in your gut, so you ignore it and do what you think you're supposed to do. The deeper mind knows, though. My family didn't talk about feelings much while I was growing up, just as I don't think my parents' families talked about feelings much, but Lilith left a mark on me when I began to scratch my arm with pushpins. For years, the scars on my arm were marks of shame, daily reminders of how bad things had once gotten. But as I learned what witchcraft was and settled gradually into a witch's life, they—like the scars from my birthmarks—became marks of survival. I had survived. My past had left a cruel kind of sigil on me, but I had survived.

Trauma after trauma after trauma, passed down along family lines until it erupts in a child with the Devil's mark sewn into her skin. Maybe the witch is a being who exists on two registers at once: the descendent of the Nephilim, claimed by Lilith and marked by the Devil, and a neglected kid slogging through depression while getting fried by UV rays. Both stories can be true. Both realities, the mythical and the mundane, can resonate and reinforce each other. As above, so below.

A few years ago, I went to see a solar eclipse and brought some tools and powders to consecrate to Lilith. As I lay my things on the grass during totality to soak up the eclipse's power, I heard a voice. "Now you are a demon," it said. The voice wasn't judgmental or unfriendly. It was practical, matter-of-fact.

Because "What is a demon?" is as interesting a question as "What is a witch?" What does it mean to be a demon, metaphorically or archetypally or literally or otherwise? What does it mean to bear the Devil's mark, to carry an eldritch bloodline? The demon, I think, is one who refuses to submit to arbitrary authority. The demon leaps from the comfortable stasis of Heaven to the grinding, churning cauldron of Earth, which grants the powers of change and free will. Demons embrace that choice and harness it. So do witches.

But to be a witch is also to be, at times, very lonely. One traditional name for witch is "hedge rider," one who straddles the hedgerow to live in both the civilized world and the wilderness. Having the witch blood means that your closest friends may live in the Otherworld while you have trouble connecting with other humans. It's a mistake to romanticize the path of the half blood, with one foot in each world and their full weight in neither. Is Lilith lonely as she flies through the night? Is the Devil lonely, searching for witches to mark and woo? They may be.

As I write this, it's time to schedule my dermatologist appointment. I have to call the doctor in the morning. I have to make sure that I catch any melanoma early, because now I have two daughters of my own whom I wanted and I love very much, and I don't want to inflict on them the trauma of a dead mother. The very mark that gave me life—true life, in which I was free to become fully myself and fly through the night—could make me an early ancestor. The Devil is a trickster, after all. Not out of malice or evil, but because nature itself is a web of balance that can look, to our human eyes, like a bag of tricks.

Are you afraid of the Devil and all their infernal hosts? Are you afraid of the demons who creep and soar in the dark? Don't be. They live in you as much as they live in me, and they're made in the image of the Divine. Search your body, search your mind and your spirit, and you may find that you already carry a secret amulet. You may find your chthonic and instinctual self, wriggling like a larva, hungry and impatient. Don't shy away. Its face is your face, its call your call, its magic the source of your deepest, most powerful magic.

At least, that's how it was for me, although it's taken me a lifetime to see it.

## A Spell to Make Your Mark

The sigil that marks your power is under your skin, written in the folds of your brain, inscribed in the marrow of your bones, stretched across the fibers of your flesh. You just haven't uncovered it yet. But it's finished now, after a lifetime of design, and it's time for you to take a look.

Getting to your mark is easy: Simply close your eyes and enter your own body. Journey inside yourself like a traveler. Walk the architecture of your skeleton and sail the exhilarating rapids of your blood. Pay attention to your surroundings, because you'll see signs telling you where to go. Some of those signs may be written in a language you already understand. Some of them may be written in something new, letters and symbols you've never seen before, carefully put there by your distant ancestors or your far-off descendants. Listen to their words. Puzzle out their messages. After all, they put them here for you to find.

You'll probably want to do a little tidying as you go. Are there old wounds you're carrying with you? Scar tissue that can be gently cleared away, or lumps of mended bone that can be smoothed and soothed? Listen to the sounds your body makes as you journey inside it. Listen to its voices and its songs. Listen for the songs of pain and try to sing a corresponding song of healing. Listen for the songs of healing so that you can take them with you when you leave.

At last, you'll find a hidden place—in the chambers of your heart, perhaps, or the ventricles of your brain. Someone put this room here for you. Is it made of bone or soft tissue? Is it hard to pry open or easy to enter? It's okay if the door has grown rusted after all these years of waiting. Brush away the detritus, and the hinges will give.

Uh-oh. You thought your mark would be waiting for you inside, didn't you? But it's not quite as simple as that. Instead, you'll find a tool with which to *make* your mark. It's your job to gather the parts of the sigil that live in your body. It's your job to combine them into a thing of power.

But here's the good news: You gathered those pieces along your journey. They followed you to this chamber. Just look around you and you'll find them. Use the tool to give your mark shape and form.

It's beautiful. It's perfect. It's your mark, and looking at it, you'll realize that it's just as familiar as your name. But your mark comes with a warning: When you wear it, you'll be recognized. A sigil is a thing of responsibility, so don't be surprised when someone notices it. Don't be surprised when they ask you for help. The magic you offer will be your mark on a broader scale, a mark that heals the world around you.

# 2

# Antler Queens

## When Hollywood awakens
## the witch blood

### Part 1: Nancy

In tenth grade, I saw a friend of mine flipping through a catalog full of velvet dresses and silver jewelry as we made our way into the choir room. When I asked what the catalog was, she told me it was for witches. She was, she explained, a witch.

"You mean you worship Satan?" I asked.

She was obviously prepared for this line of questioning. I may have been the tenth person to ask her that day. "No!" she said. "That's a myth. Witches worship nature."

Velvet dresses and silver jewelry sounded great, but it was the part about nature that took me aback. I had a sudden vision of my friend dressed in a simple brown shawl, kneeling before an altar in a forest. The image arose fully formed, and my mental image of a witch hasn't changed much in the decades since then. It felt like catching a glimpse of a past life, or an alternate one. An awakened ancestral memory. A brief rip in the multiverse. I decided that I was a witch, too.

It's possible that if I'd grown up somewhere else, I would have found my way to witchcraft much earlier, and in a more romantic way than a catalog. When I was ten days old, my parents moved from Los Angeles to the suburbs of Orange County, crossing a barrier known as the Orange Curtain. Los Angeles is progressive and cosmopolitan, with a weird and winding history of alternative churches and occult societies. It was near Los Angeles that rocket scientist Jack Parsons planned the infamous Babalon Working, in which he tried to incarnate the Thelemite goddess Babalon in human form. It's Los Angeles that's home to Hermetic and Masonic temples and countless occult shops.

Orange County, on the other hand, is known for its ultraconservative Christians. At my school, my biology teacher skipped the unit on evolution, and my English teacher told us the book of Genesis was historical fact. Up in Berkeley, my future sisters-in-law learned about historical witches in school. In Orange County, I didn't know real witches existed.

Still, the Evangelicals couldn't control everything, and bits of information got past the curtain. Wicca, the neopagan religion invented in the 1950s by occultist Gerald Gardner, enjoyed a revival in the '90s, bolstered by the witchy aesthetic of artists like Tori Amos. One day, at a bookshop near Cal State Fullerton, I discovered one small shelf labeled New Age. On that shelf I discovered one book called *The Practice of Witchcraft Today*. Its author was Robin Skelton, and its cover bore a deliciously occult-looking illustration from a 19th-century astrology book.

Over the next few days, I devoured the book in secret. It described something called the Old Religion: a belief system, transmitted in an unbroken chain of secret devotees dating back to neolithic Europe, that venerated a mother goddess and her horned or antlered consort. The goddess gave birth to the horned god at the winter solstice, the book said, and then slept with him in spring before he died in the fall. The book contained spells for making plants grow, easing menstrual pain, and binding someone with a photograph. The copyright date was 1990, but I felt like I was holding something ancient in my hands. I memorized the names of the eight annual holy days known as Sabbats. I lit candles on full moons and made an altar pentacle out of modeling clay. I took the book with me to school each day, discreetly tucked in with my textbooks. I was parched for something I'd never been able to name, and that book finally nourished me.

Much of what Wiccans believed in the '90s turned out to be what witches now call "fakelore." There's no secret chain of initiates dating back thousands of years. The Goddess and Horned God are based more on the work of the mid–20th century author Robert Graves than any single prehistoric religion. There are kernels of truth to it, though. There are the scattered myths and folktales of Britain and Ireland, which carry memories of something much older. There's the "fairy faith" of pre-Christian Europe, in which people claimed to see dead relatives in the Fairy Queen's court. The fakelore of Wicca touched spiritual seekers not because it was seductive, but because it pointed the way to something real.

Still, it's hard to build an entire spiritual practice out of just one paperback, especially with something as experiential as witchcraft. To really grok witchcraft, you have to get up, shake off your torpor, and do it. The obvious thing to do would have been to ask my friend if she wanted to practice with me, but we weren't that close, and—for reasons I'd understand much later in life—there was always some inscrutable barrier between me and other people. I just couldn't bring myself to do it. I called myself a witch, but really it felt like I aspired to be a witch. I got a copy of my friend's catalog, but jewelry didn't seem like the answer. Witchcraft felt like something always on the horizon, something beautiful and vital, something that I was journeying toward but could never quite reach.

Then, a few months after I got my book, I saw a movie called *The Craft*.

*The Craft* is cynical, campy, and offensive, and to this day it's one of my favorite movies. It tried to cash in on a spiritual fad and ended up raising a generation of witches instead.

The plot: Sarah, a teenage girl recovering from a suicide attempt, moves to LA with her father and stepmother. There are three witches at her Catholic school—Nancy, Bonnie, and Rochelle—and they immediately recognize Sarah as the fourth member of their coven, the last piece of the puzzle they need to make their magic work. Together, the girls work spells to get what they want and exact revenge against the people who have wronged them, but when Nancy finds a grimoire with instructions for taking the witch god Manon into herself, she's driven insane with power. Sarah has to stop her, fighting a volley of horrific glamours and illusions so that she can strip the entire coven of their magic.

Before I saw the movie, I tried some of the rituals from my book, sitting in front of a bookshelf I'd converted into an altar. The workings were written for groups, but I adapted them, calling in the four elements, casting a magic circle, and speaking the invocations. Nothing felt right. I was always keenly aware of myself, in my bedroom, whispering words to nothing. It felt hokey, like playing pretend. Where was the magic? Where was the mysticism I'd experienced as a child?

Sarah and her friends, on the other hand—*they make magic*. In their first working as a group, they perform a sort of dedication ritual, and they're rewarded with a gentle cloud of butterflies. When Nancy invokes Manon, she shouts incantations into a lightning storm, her arms thrown up to channel her power. The movie *crackles* with magic. Years later, I found out that the filmmakers hired an actual Wiccan consultant to write the rituals and that consultant used language that dates back to the 19th-century Hermetic Order of the Golden Dawn. Why do the girls' rituals sound so good? It could be because the Golden Dawn counted writers like William Butler Yeats among its members. After I saw the movie, I hurriedly wrote down the girls' prayers and invocations and tried them myself. *Hail to the Guardians of the Watchtowers of the North.* Better. Much better.

The best part of *The Craft*, though, are the film's settings. Sarah and the others visit a dreamy little occult store, staffed by the gauzy priestess Lirio, to buy their candles and books. Their initiation is held in a dappled oak woodland. Nancy performs her invocation at a beach with sea caves. The movie is gorgeous.

My hometown, by contrast, was violently stripped of its natural landscape. Southern California is home to gentle hills of chaparral and breathtaking fields of wildflowers, coniferous forests in the mountains and tide pools brimming with life. Brush your hand against any of our sages, and their scent will fill the air, peppery and sweet. Look closely, and you'll see Anna's hummingbirds and monarch butterflies drinking from the fuschia and milkweed. Hawks and owls glide overhead while mountain lions amble through the forests. California in its natural state feels like Eden.

Thanks to developers, though, Orange County was paved over and beaten into submission. Even the orange groves eventually gave way to hundreds of identical houses. There was nowhere to walk that wasn't concrete and asphalt, no plants that weren't sterile ornamentals, and no business that wasn't a chain. I longed for nature, but I didn't know how to get to it, and I was the only one who seemed to think it was worth getting to. The people of Orange County generally believed that a static, anonymous place was paradise. It felt like Hell to me.

I clearly wasn't the only one who felt penned in by the suburbs, who felt that I didn't belong. The tropes you find in *The Craft*—the misfit girls, the occult shop, the rituals, the landscape—are a microcosm of what so many of us wanted in the '90s. Before she meets Nancy and the others, Sarah knows there's something sacred and important missing from her life, and its absence nearly kills her. But she finds a family in her coven, who show her a beautiful, hidden world in which her innate power can be cultivated. They initiate her into their sacred mysteries and form a tight circle of female friendship. They can access natural beauty: the forest grove with the butterflies, the rocky beach, the herbs hanging from the walls of Lirio's shop.

But it's telling that Sarah's journey begins in a shop, instead of a library or a community or a temple. Lirio sells Sarah a book with instructions on how to do witchcraft, and the girls' altars are all piled with knickknacks. All of us teen witches wanted something real and transformative, but the only way we knew how to call it in was by buying things.

Nevertheless, in *The Craft*, I saw the life I'd been aching for—a life of magic, deep in the green. Yes, I found out about that life by going to the movies instead of going to the wilderness. But notice that I was *able* to access it that way. *The Craft* showed me a path that years later would lead to something wild and bloody and beautiful. Art, like magic, can't help but seep up from the cracks.

My mom eventually found my book. She also found my pentacle necklace, which I carried in a pouch in my backpack. I was afraid she'd take them away, but instead she grimly gave me a Bible.

Then a Borders Books opened nearby, the biggest bookstore I'd ever seen in my life. On our first visit, I wandered, wide-eyed, through the aisles, taking in the thousands of spines and covers arrayed around me. Instead of one small New Age shelf, I found an entire section—I'm talking like *three whole bookshelves!*—devoted to witchcraft and paganism. There were enough books to keep me busy for months. Scott Cunningham, Starhawk, Laurie Cabot, Gerina Dunwich, Silver Ravenwolf, Ann Moura—all the authors of the '90s Wiccan revival poured out like water from a fountain, and I drank them up.

At least, I tried to. In the '80s and '90s, witches bent over backward to present themselves to the public as respectable. Every book cited the Wiccan Rede—"An it harm none, do as ye will"—while witches like Laurie Cabot suggested visiting city council meetings to assure your neighbors that you wouldn't eat their babies. The Satanic Panic was in full swing, with frenzied mobs throwing around accusations of ritual murder. Child Protective Services was reportedly taking people's kids away. Even as late as 2013, a friend of mine encountered an adoption agency that didn't allow witchcraft in the homes of prospective families.

In the end, the result of the Wiccan PR campaign wasn't widespread acceptance of witchcraft. Instead, it was widespread ridicule. No one fears the witch anymore, because the witch is someone who blows their money on quartz crystals and airbrushed paintings of fairies. No one fears the witch, because they're too busy laughing at us. I may have had a vague inkling of this problem as a teen, buying all those books from Borders, but I didn't know enough to recognize it. Instead, I accepted a witchcraft that was declawed and defanged, and wondered why it never felt quite right.

In *The Craft*, though, Sarah and her coven aren't harmless at all. A racist White girl harasses Rochelle, so Rochelle makes the girl's hair fall out. Nancy's dad is abusive, so Nancy gives him a heart attack. A boy tries to rape Sarah, so Nancy telekinetically launches him out a window. Nowadays, younger generations of witches point out that folk magic has always been a tool of the oppressed and disenfranchised: women, people of color, people in poverty. Magic is what you use when you don't have access to money or power. The coven in *The Craft* uses their power to strike back against patriarchy and White supremacy.

But in the movie, it's that very power that ruins Nancy, leaving her a babbling wreck, tied to a hospital bed. It's better for everyone, the movie is careful to remind us, when teen girls are powerless. See how destructive girls are when they band together? See how orderly everything is when they're separated? Just look at what happens when they forget their place.

I graduated high school, escaped Orange County and flew away to a little college in New York that had a pagan group. Once a month we would hold a meeting at which we dutifully cast the circle, called the elements, and invoked whatever gods we felt like working with. (That right there—that casual attitude toward gods—was one sign that most of us didn't really believe in what we were doing.) We read each other's cards and gave every couple in the group a Wiccan hand-fasting. We bickered a lot. Some members claimed they could control the weather. The group eventually split into warring factions and then fell apart.

But. But. There were wild places on campus. An old stone stairway that led to a hidden grove. A patch of undeveloped land that held deer paths. Slowly I began to dip my toe into the green. One night, I dreamt that everyone in the world had antlers, but we all shaved them down each morning. Walking through the grass in the quad, I decided to let my antlers grow out. No dream before that had ever felt so right.

## Part 2: Lottie

Over the years, I've bought *The Craft* on VHS, DVD, and Prime Video. No matter what media I'm using, I always make sure I have a copy on hand.

These days, though, I've been watching the series *Yellowjackets*. If you weren't a teen girl in the '90s, you may not notice the connection between the two—but if you were, it's easy to see their shared DNA. Instead of a coven, *Yellowjackets* focuses on a 1996 girls' soccer team, stranded in the wilderness after a plane crash. Instead of the deity Manon, there's a nameless god in the forest, protecting the girls and demanding sacrifices in exchange. Instead of seaside invocations, the girls practice blood magic and cannibalism.

I'll admit that my interest wavered throughout most of season 1, but the episode that got me hooked was "Doomcoming." In this episode, the girls, having lived in the woods for months, judge from the weather that it must be around Homecoming time. They each happened to pack a nice dress for the reception they were going to attend at Nationals before the plane crash, so they decide to put on a dance outside of the abandoned cabin where they're living.

Like *The Craft*, *Yellowjackets* benefits from amazing sets and costumes. The girls somehow dredge up yards of ribbon and lace to decorate the woods. (I suppose some of the lace is actually soccer nets, but those girls work wonders with it.) They make stunning flower crowns and garlands. Way back in the first episode, we see a flash-forward to an antlered figure eating the flesh of a murdered girl, and during Doomcoming, a girl named Lottie dons an antlered crown. Lottie becomes what fans quickly dubbed the Antler Queen.

What is it about antlers that's so arresting? Why did I dream about them? Why does the goddess's consort wear them? Why is Lottie's transformation so immediate and awe-inspiring when she puts them on? In many streams of modern witchcraft, antlers and horns symbolize divine wisdom, stretching to the heavens to pour knowledge into the wearer's mind. To the witch, horned gods like Cernunnos and Pan represent, among other things, the insights that are found in liminality, the unmapped borderlands between animal and human, Earth and sky, male and female. Antlers are usually associated with masculinity, but female reindeer grow them, and the Bucca of traditional witchcraft is seen by many witches as androgyne. In *Old World Witchcraft*, Raven Grimassi sees the god and goddess of the witches in the image of antler-like tree branches growing around the pregnant moon. In *Craft of the Untamed*, Nicholaj de Mattos Frisvold compares horns and antlers to divine lightning rods, enabling the transmission of wisdom from the vastness of the cosmos. In ritual, many witches don a horned or antlered headdress. In *The Craft*, Nancy is literally struck by lightning when she invokes Manon.

At first, the *Yellowjackets'* Doomcoming dance seems to go well. Little do the girls know, though, that there are hallucinogenic mushrooms in their stew. Suddenly the dance turns into a hunt. Like the women of Thebes in *The Bacchae*, driven into a frenzy by Dionysus, the girls begin to chase their coach's son Travis. When they catch him, they nearly slit his throat. Deep in the woods, the girls become wild and ferocious, with the Antler Queen presiding over them.

Like Nancy in *The Craft*, Lottie in *Yellowjackets* is plugged into something mysterious and awe-inspiring. When her antipsychotic medication runs out, she starts having visions, and soon she's acting as a spiritual leader for the other girls. She leaves a bear's heart by a tree as an offering to the forest god, and uses a blood sacrifice to keep Shauna from dying in childbirth. Like Nancy, Lottie is portrayed as dangerous and unnatural. (I mean, yes, the cannibalism isn't great, but it's winter and there's no food!) When we catch up with her years later, she's terrified of her own power, trying to suppress it by running a pathologically bland wellness cult.

But we know the truth about Lottie, and Nancy, and all the girls around them. They're bloody. Witches are bloody. Magic is *bloody*. In the woods, among the old gods, the body blooms with blood as the mind unravels in terrible ecstasy. When those of us with the witch blood see our antler queens, even on the screen, we recognize them as life-giving. Dangerous, yes. Monstrous, absolutely. But so intensely life-giving.

Here's what I didn't understand in my early days of studying witchcraft: Memorized invocations and store-bought tools aren't enough. They never got me back to the spontaneous visions and epiphanies that I had as a child. When you let your antlers grow out—when you truly open yourself to the old powers—your claws and teeth come out, too. To tamp down this power when it calls to you is to smother your witch fire before it ever has a chance to catch.

I wish I could describe what growing antlers feels like, how to get it to happen, how you know when you've done it right. What can I say? Maybe this: The world is suddenly sharper and more real. You snap into attunement and leave your skin behind. It feels like being touched by lightning.

For a long time after college, I gave up on witchcraft completely. I spent years studying other traditions: secular Buddhism, a little Hinduism, my own Jewish heritage. But the witch blood still pulsed in me.

I lived in New York, San Francisco, Paris, and Iowa City. Eventually, I settled back down in Los Angeles, where I found out that Fairuza Balk, who played Nancy, owned an occult shop in Hollywood called Panpipes. She'd gone there for research while filming *The Craft* and saved it from being turned into a restaurant.

I went there on a Sunday at 1 p.m., and although the store's website said it opened at one on Sundays, the place was shuttered. The shop was a few blocks from Hollywood and Vine, surrounded by tourist traps and adult video stores, and I'd paid $2 for an hour of meter parking and felt like I'd been tricked. There was a farmer's market down the street, so I wandered down to it and bought some herbal tea. The meter ticked. I went back to the store at 1:40, and there was a sign on the door saying, BACK IN 5 MINUTES, and a young woman waiting outside.

"She's probably doing a reading," the woman said. Fairuza Balk!? "No," she said. "Vicky. She runs the place." I fretted that the meter would run out. "Don't you have quarters?" she asked. Well, yes, but . . . I couldn't figure out how to explain that I was embarrassed to be here, that I had never managed to truly find my way into witchcraft, that deep down I feared that the critics were right and all this stuff was a waste of time.

Then the woman introduced herself and asked what I practiced. I didn't know what to say. I wanted to have an answer.

At that moment, the door opened, and a woman with pink hair let us in. I was surprised at how disappointed I was. The woman outside had been so nice, so easy to talk to. I would have enjoyed finding out what she practiced.

She started talking to the shopkeeper about an herbal bath that hadn't worked right, and I wandered around to take everything in. The shop had some books, some candles, some jewelry—nothing that I particularly wanted. But being there felt like a way back in.

Later, I found out that the filming locations for *The Craft* are scattered around Los Angeles. Sarah's crumbling Spanish-style house is in Sunland. The apartment that served as Lirio's store is in Thai Town. And the sea caves! The sea caves are real. They weren't a green screen.

They're up the coast a ways, on a public beach. You can go there if you like.

Around the time I went to Panpipes, I had my first baby, and the bloodiness of birth—the bloodiness and milkiness and holiness of becoming a mother to a daughter—helped to awaken my witch blood again. One day, I went to Nancy's beach, climbing over rocks until I found a hidden place to perform a simple rite on the sand. Before me lay the sea; behind me were hills of manzanita, where owls called and bobcats prowled and rabbits cautiously grazed in the twilight.

I suddenly smelled the musk of deer on the wind. My mind crackled. I was home.

Nancy always deserved a home. She deserved access to divinity and power. Instead, she ends up living out her days in an asylum. As I write this, *Yellowjackets* still has three seasons to go, but so far, Lottie isn't faring much better.

"Over time, we have seen the feminine instinctive nature looted, driven back, and overbuilt," writes Clarissa Pinkola Estés in her seminal work *Women Who Run with the Wolves*. "For long periods it has been mismanaged like the wildlife and the wildlands. For several thousand years, as soon and as often as we turn our backs, it is relegated to the poorest land in the psyche. The spiritual lands of Wild Woman have, throughout history, been plundered or burnt, dens bulldozed, and natural cycles forced into unnatural rhythms to please others." This catastrophic loss of women's divinity and women's stories has occurred in most of the cultures that Westerners like me will ever encounter. No wonder stories of witches are so magnetic. *The Craft,*

*Yellowjackets, The Wicker Man, Practical Magic, The Love Witch, The Witch: A New England Folktale*—we devour stories of dangerous women. We're starved. We need nourishment.

We need our antler queens—wholly realized, undiminished, and with their power intact. When will they come?

---

## A Spell to Grow Your Antlers

Your antlers are made of your home, so start there.

First, you'll need to travel to the wildest place you know. This is the place where you've felt the heartbeat of the Earth, where you've seen its pulse in the soil. This is the place where the elements entangle into a beautiful chaos, a nexus of life. Go to that place and meet its guardian. Listen to what they tell you. Do what they ask. When they give you a gift, accept it.

Next, you'll need to go to the most sterile place you know. This is the place where the land has been silenced, where its life has been suppressed, where the raucous calls of the spirits have been smothered and forgotten. There's still magic here. Magic always finds the cracks and breaks through. Gather the hidden strength of this place. Its steward may slip you some through a hidden passage, careful not to be seen.

After that, gather strength from the purest place you know, the place that washes you clean. It'll take something from you that you thought you needed, maybe even something you thought was part of you. But the guardian of this place is wise. Listen to them.

And after that go to the dirtiest place, the place that reeks of rot and decay. I won't lie—the guardian of this place is hard to get along with. But they may give you the most valuable gift of all.

Go to the lowest place you know, the place that dips almost to the hidden fire in the Earth. Touch the ground to gather its strength. The steward of this place will whisper to you through the bedrock.

Then go to the highest place, the place where the air is thin and cold. Stretch up to the sky to gather strength here. Don't fear the guardian's talons—they know you're a friend.

Six places, six directions, six tines for your burgeoning antlers. Go to your altar with the strength you've gathered from the land, and lay it around you to let it sink into the soil. When it's ready, cured and composted and reformed as roots, it will push up through the soles of your feet.

Your antlers don't just sprout from your skull. Of course not! They're an extension of your bones, of the temple of your skeleton, and you'll feel them forming from your feet up through your spine. Let them rise from the Earth through your blood. Don't shy away from the power they bring you. Don't shy away from all the different facets of your home. To grow your antlers, you'll need to embrace every part of the land that has made you, from the healthiest parts to the sickliest, the most beautiful to the most rotten. Take them into you. It'll be okay.

You'll feel your antlers push through the crown of your head as they drink in the stars. This is part of the magic, too. Don't shy away.

Roots below, antlers above: Now you're tethered to the Great Above and the Great Below, tethered to the land around you, your roots reaching to each horizon. To be regal, to be a witch, is to be tethered to the land you serve. You'll never be free again, and yet you're freer than you've ever been before.

# 3

## My Mother's Tarot

### On card games and divination as sacred play

My mother would never call herself an antler queen, but she did dabble in magic.

Growing up, I had a bad habit of rifling through her closet while she was at work. In my defense, she had some really cool stuff in there: vintage sweaters and costume jewelry from the '70s, a rhinestone-studded dress she'd gone dancing in before the divorce, diaries from when she was a teenager. One day, I unearthed an old tarot deck and guidebook. The deck was labeled TAROK NO. IJJ.

"What's this?" I asked, bringing it to her. The illustrations on the cards were old-timey etchings, like the Renaissance-era art I'd seen at the Met during a trip back east. The copyright date was 1969, and the cardstock was soft and brittle. One card was labeled Junon, showing the goddess in a toga and crown with a peacock at her feet. Another depicted Jupiter, reclining in his throne. J and J.

My mom had long since given up telling me to stay out of her closet, so when she saw the deck, she just shrugged. "Oh, I got those years ago."

"But *why?*" I asked, dumbfounded. I thought of all the televangelists she'd made us watch over the years. Every Easter she talked about going to a sunrise service, but we never made it. Instead, she'd turn on the broadcast from the nearby Crystal Cathedral. She hated my growing collection of books on witchcraft. She hated the altar tools that kept arriving in the mail. And now I was finding tarot cards in her closet? What *was* this?

Her voice took on the slightest edge, as if I'd asked a stupid question. "Well, because I thought I'd use them."

And she refused to say any more.

My mother has never liked talking about her past, so I don't know much about her life before she got pregnant with me. Here's what I do know: She spent the first years of her life in the Bronx, before my grandfather used his salary as a mailman to buy land in Dobbs Ferry and build a mail-order Sears house there. After my grandmother died, my grandfather married a woman my mother hated. My mom finished college around 1970 and moved to New York City, where she hung out in Greenwich Village. Then she went to San Francisco, started dating a Jewish dental student, and followed him when he returned to his hometown of Los Angeles. There they got pregnant with me.

Growing up, I always thought of my mother as solidly mainstream, a lover of game shows and buffet restaurants. She liked to call out the answers to questions on *Wheel of Fortune* and *Jeopardy!* She worked as an accountant before she went to law school. But her vinyl collection was amazing. She had the Grateful Dead and Joan Baez and Janis Joplin's *Cheap Thrills*, with the iconic R. Crumb cover that fascinated me long before I knew who R. Crumb was. Once, in one of my excursions into her closet, I found an old photo of her decked out in full hippie regalia: floral shirt, beads, golden locks tumbling down her shoulders. I stared, riveted. Then, in one of those childhood blunders for which you never forgive yourself, I told her how beautiful she'd once been. She told me to put the photo away.

Greenwich Village in the '70s. Can you imagine? The clothes, the music, the vibes? My mom told me there was a band in a tiny club that covered Jefferson Airplane's "White Rabbit" every single night. God, what I'd give to spend one day exploring that scene. I'm positive that that's where she got her tarot deck.

If you pick up a book on the history of tarot, you'll notice an odd tendency. Historians devote a lot of time to the development of the Rider-Waite (now more commonly known as the Smith-Waite) in 1909, and rightly so. Created by Golden Dawn members Arthur Waite and Pamela Colman Smith, the Smith-Waite infused what had largely been a simple card game with occult imagery. The Popess card became the High Priestess; the Juggler became the robed and infinity-crowned Magician. People had used tarot cards for fortune telling before, but the Smith-Waite was one of the first decks to be created by and for mystics. There were others—the 1789 Book of Thoth tarot, for instance—but the Smith-Waite was the most successful and enduring.

After the birth of the Smith-Waite, the history of tarot seems to present a smooth ride from 19th-century Hermeticism to the 1970s New Age movement. When tarot became an occult tool, it seems, no one ever looked back. I personally never questioned that version of events—after all, it made intuitive sense. Plus, that history gets cemented a little more every time you see a Smith-Waite deck for sale. It's generally considered the flagship deck for U.S. Games Systems, the company that publishes many of the tarot decks in the United States. There are too many versions of the Smith-Waite to count. It's synonymous with tarot.

Because of that history, I always assumed that my mother's strange little 1JJ deck, with its unfortunate name and antiquated artwork, was some obscure, short-lived offshoot. After all, the only copy of it I'd ever seen was my own. Imagine my surprise when I found out that the 1JJ was instrumental in the rise of modern American tarot.

It started in Germany in 1968, when Wall Street businessman Stuart Kaplan—future founder of U.S. Games Systems—visited the Nuremberg Toy Fair looking for games to import to the US as a side business. At the fair, there was a booth run by a playing card company, AG Müller and Cie, and tucked into the far corner was one lonely tarot deck. Not the Smith-Waite, though. The 1JJ.

The deck was probably used for the Swiss card games Troccas and Troggu, and AG Müller and Cie was floored when Kaplan ordered five thousand copies—more than they sold in a year—for the US market. Kaplan then wrote a guidebook, *Tarot Cards for Fun and Fortune Telling*, teaching people how to perform a reading.

Of course, tarot wasn't unknown in America in the sixty years between the debut of the Smith-Waite and Kaplan's discovery of the 1JJ. The characters on the TV series *Dark Shadows* did some readings here and there, Eden Gray's *The Tarot Revealed* came out in 1960, and Sylvia Plath's "Daddy" contains a reference to the "Taroc pack." But AG Müller and Cie were right to be taken aback by Kaplan's interest, because tarot seems to have been a fringe activity at best, and even Kaplan, despite his piqued interest, had never heard of it before he stumbled upon the 1JJ.

He had the right instinct, though. New Age thought and alternative spiritual practices had swept the country. The 1JJ was a huge success, selling over two hundred thousand copies and inspiring Kaplan to form U.S. Games Systems. Years later, he acquired the rights to the Smith-Waite.

When I first learned this history in a biography of Kaplan, I felt like I'd somersaulted into a new reality. One of the first bookstores to sell the 1JJ, according to the sources I found, was Brentano's, which had New York locations in White Plains and Greenwich Village. My mother may have bought her deck at either of those stores. I imagined her opening the tuck box after leaving the store, shuffling her new novelty, and laying out her first spread. Did she just get a tarot deck because it was trendy? Because all her friends were doing it and she wanted to fit in, despite the specter of her Christian family's shame? Or did it feel good and right to her, like a key clicking snugly into a lock, the way witchcraft did for me? When she stopped using her cards, was it because she'd returned to the spiritual life she wanted, or did she bury a part of herself forever?

Maybe tarot was just a game to her, a passing fancy that she soon grew bored with. Or maybe it was something more. If I hadn't found those cards in her closet, that chapter of her story could have remained hidden, just like the 1JJ.

Once I had my mother's tarot cards, the obvious next step was learning how to read them.

The Celtic Cross spread, consisting of ten cards laid out in a six-card cross with a five-card column next to it, is probably the worst possible spread to learn if you've never read cards before. Ten cards give you a *lot* to interpret, especially when the position of each card in the spread adds its own layer of meaning. Nevertheless, the booklet that came with the 1JJ prescribed it, so that's what I went with.

What made it even harder was the fact that the 1JJ is a variant of the Tarot of Marseilles. The Smith-Waite has a full illustration on each card, which makes readings vastly easier. Even if you're not familiar with all the occult correspondences of swords or pentacles, even if you can't read Hebrew letters or you don't recognize Enochian imagery, the scene on each Smith-Waite card turns a three-card spread into a little comic strip or storyboard. You can imagine a person hopping from card to card, changing props and costumes as they go: They sit regally on their throne as the Queen of Wands, then abdicate and flee in the Six of Swords, before dancing joyfully in a simpler life in the Ten of Cups. The Smith-Waite was designed for divination, and the cards want to be read.

Not so with the Tarot of Marseilles. Instead of illustrated scenes, the minor arcana are pip cards. The Ten of Cups, for example, just depicts ten cups, which is much less expressive than the Smith-Waite's drawing of children dancing under a rainbow. There are systems that readers use to interpret pip cards—more on that in a bit—but I didn't know that when I sat down with my 1JJ cards as a teenager. The booklet didn't even bother with the pips ("Hoo boy, you're on your own with those," Kaplan seemed to be saying), instructing readers to just work with the trumps. But I didn't want to do that. I didn't want shortcuts. So I made a fatal mistake: I turned to a list of card interpretations in one of my witchcraft books and tried to memorize all seventy-eight of them.

Between that, the Celtic Cross, and my idea that you were supposed to ask the cards simple yes-or-no questions about the future, my readings were about as insightful as a broken Magic 8 Ball. "Will I get a boyfriend this year?" I'd ask. Ten cards later, I'd have a teetering pile of information about "prudence" and "an older woman" and "folly" and "imminent betrayal" and "a sudden financial opportunity" and nothing resembling a sensible answer to my question.

I put the cards away for a while. Eventually, I bought a Smith-Waite variant—the Mage: The Ascension, which I found out about from a friend who was into role-playing games—but even with the illustrations to help me, I ran up against the same walls. I tried to memorize seventy-eight meanings instead of just looking at what the cards depicted. I used ridiculously complicated spreads. I put those cards away, too, and didn't attempt tarot again for a long time.

How did a card game turn into a fortune-telling tool, and then a vehicle for spiritual work? The evolution of tarot wasn't inevitable, when you think about it.

People have come up with false histories, of course. Some are convinced that the secrets of ancient Egyptian magic are encoded in the cards. Others have tried to link the tarot to mystical traditions like the Jewish Kabbalah. In reality, the tarot was created in 15th-century Italy. Any spiritual resonances—the Pope and Popess, for example, or the four apostles on the World card—were simply window dressing for a Christian society. There are dozens of different tarot games, and over the centuries, the tarot evolved into modern-day playing cards.

Does that mean that tarot is meaningless? It's easy to see why occultists would want to create alternate histories for the tarot. It may feel crass to admit that your spiritual system comes from cards that Italian nobles tossed down on their lacquered tables on a rainy day. Sometimes, when I was learning tarot, I'd fantasize that my mother was a cunning woman who gave me my cards in a secret ceremony instead of a tax lawyer who'd stuffed an old curio in her closet.

But isn't the point of divination to get at the truth of things? To peel away delusion and falsehood? So let's get at it, then. Let's stop veering away from a truth that, in its way, is just as meaningful as the stories we've been told.

Cunning folk and conjure workers didn't have access to leather-bound grimoires, consecrated swords, or crystal balls. If they needed to work a spell, they would see what they had around the house. If they needed to predict the future or give someone advice, they would consult the tools that were available. Maybe playing cards, maybe bones, maybe the birds migrating overhead. Some of witchcraft's most beautiful folk traditions come from simple practices like these. They've never been fancy. They've never needed to be.

Really, it's not that different from me getting my religion from a movie. Our spirits can't help but look past the mundane. We strain to find meaning in ordinary objects. A card game seems to hide a secret, spiritual world, like the veil lifted from a humdrum landscape to reveal the glittering Otherworld behind it.

Isn't that clever of our ancestors? Their ingenuity should make you proud.

*Witch Blood Rising*

Of course, even deeper than the question of *why we read tarot is the question of how we do it. How does tarot work?*

Because even after I'd given up on trying to learn it the first time, I saw it work. I went to a party at which a reader casually turned over card after card, describing my love life to me as if she were reading my diary. I was careful not to feed her too much information—I knew that people could get scammed—but the words spilled out of her, unhurried yet abundant. The cards were clearly telling her my story. Maybe you just had to be psychic, I thought.

Many years later, I found my *Mage: The Ascension Tarot* deck and started playing with it again. Again, I tried to memorize the card meanings, flipping through books instead of looking at the illustrations right in front of me. Again, I couldn't do it.

Then, one night, with my newborn finally asleep in her cradle, I got tired of that approach. I paused in the middle of shuffling the cards, and instead of laying them out in the Celtic Cross, I spread three in a row. Before me lay a little tableau, actors performing a scene. I softly narrated the story they told, and then shuffled the deck again.

This time, I tried a question. "When will we find a new apartment?" I asked. The story unspooled—again, meaningless, overly complicated, and completely unhelpful. I swept the cards back up and tried again, this time with a question that was more open-ended, one that invited me to take control of the situation. "We need a bigger apartment," I said. "What should we do?" Now the cards started talking.

The secret to reading the cards, I realized, was to scheme with them like a co-conspirator instead of trying to operate them like a time machine. Ask them the kind of question they want to answer, the kind that lets them tell you a story. Treat tarot like a game, and the cards will play with you. Tarot can be profound in the same way that any story is profound, because even if the story is quotidian on the surface, it contains hidden wisdom. A tarot reading is an allegory, a parable, a fable, a riddle. Like a sacred drama, it knocks you out of ordinary reality and opens you up to truths your conscious mind may have missed.

After I changed my reading style, I started reading for other people. My workplace held a holiday craft fair, and I offered three-card spreads for a dollar. One of my coworkers looked stricken as I told her the story in the cards. "Keep doing this," she breathed afterwards handing me my dollar. "You're really good at it."

As I kept reading for people, and eventually took on real, paying clients, people would gasp when they saw their truth in the cards and compliment me on my ability. But I didn't feel special. I just relayed what the cards said.

Which brings us back to the question I asked earlier: How does tarot work?

Skeptics, of course, claim that readers rely on cold-reading techniques ("I see an elderly figure. Does that remind you of anyone?" or "I see a momentous change. Tell me about it!") or simply give readings that are so vague they could apply to anything. Sure, you see a lot of that. After all, anyone can call themselves a psychic. But that doesn't explain the readings that get straight to the core of the questioner's problem or reveal information that the reader couldn't possibly guess. Once, I went to a reader and told him only that I needed help with a writing project. He gave me the word *tween* without knowing I was working on a young adult (YA) novel, and his answer solved my problem. Another time, when I was reading for a client, I showed her how every card depicted her in a warm, Mediterranean climate. Her friend smacked her on the elbow. "See?" she cried. "I'm telling you, go to Greece!"

In explaining the tarot, social worker and tarot reader Jessica Dore invokes the Jungian idea of synchronicity, in which two events create meaning for someone despite being unrelated. She argues that tarot activates ways of knowing other than pure rationality and allows us to access information we may have otherwise ignored. Tarot shows us truth in the same way that paintings, folktales, and other works of art show us truth. Once, my therapist had me put together a collage during our session, and when I finished it, I realized I'd created an image of the very problem I'd come in to talk about. What were the odds that the exact pictures I'd need to create the image would be waiting in my therapist's pile of magazines? Could I have come to the same insight if I'd found completely different pictures? Maybe, but the point is that the pictures got me there, and so does a tarot reading.

Of course, tarot is witchcraft, not just a psychological tool, and witchcraft means embracing the mysterious and unseen. Rachel Pollack, author of numerous classic books on tarot, has a more metaphysical explanation for how tarot works. She writes that a reading doesn't just feed you information, but sends ripples through the web of time to create your future—and perhaps even your past. A reading, if we follow Pollack's line of thought, functions as a sort of nexus in your timeline, a fulcrum around which other events revolve. Every reader may give a different answer for how tarot works—Intuition! Magic!

Spirit guides! Space aliens!—but they'll all agree that the cards reveal truths, that they give wise counsel to a reader who has learned to work with them.

Once, for fun, I calculated all the possible permutations in a three-card spread. (Well, I used a website to do it, but I had to learn the difference between permutations and combinations, which I didn't even know were separate things.) Assuming you're using a full seventy-eight-card deck, you could theoretically perform 456,456 readings before laying down the exact same spread twice. That's not even factoring in reversed cards. Combine that probability with the ever-growing number of decks out there, each with its own images and art style, and the number of possible readings is infinite. Of course, any reader knows that the cards are feisty and opinionated. Sometimes, the same card comes up for a reader again and again, even if they use different decks. It's not unheard of to draw a card you hate, then reshuffle, redraw, and pull the same card again. Tarot is a mystical game; it's a sophisticated tool; it's a living partner in ritual.

After I'd started reading professionally—and amassed about a dozen decks—I started to wonder where the old 1JJ had ended up. My childhood bedroom was filled with boxes. I poked around in them occasionally, but I began to search in earnest when my mom told me she was selling the house.

I went there every weekend, frantically emptying box after box, but to no avail. My mom, meanwhile, was purging bags and bags of stuff, sending some to Goodwill and putting others in the trash. What if I didn't find the deck? What if we accidentally threw it away? It wasn't like the cards were a priceless antique; you can get a deck on eBay for about $25. But they were *our* cards—my mother's and mine. Maybe someday they'd be my daughter's. I needed them, and the clock was ticking.

I was close to giving up when a member of a tarot group I attended suggested doing a reading to find them. How did I not think of that? She pulled out her Smith-Waite and drew the Emperor and the Nine of Swords. A figure on a throne, and another figure sitting up in bed, her hands over her face in worry. I remembered all my own sleepless nights in high school, my abysmal grades, my tattered mental health. Something about the Emperor's throne caught my attention. I imagined an object underneath it, tucked into a compartment behind the Emperor's legs.

I went back to my mom's house. My old desk chair was in the corner, the one I'd always sat in to stare miserably at homework that made no sense. Under the chair was a box, and inside the box was the deck.

I began to learn the art of reading the Tarot of Marseilles. Reading the scenes on the trumps and court cards is much like reading the Smith-Waite. To read the pips, though, you use a completely different method. Every number has its own meaning. The number one stands for unity, or loneliness. The number five can be a new idea, or the human body. You can come up with your own correspondences. What does a number mean to you? That's the meaning you use.[1]

Each suit also has a meaning. Swords are conflict, Cups are romance or relationships, Coins are wealth, and Wands are action.

---

1. If you want to know more about combining numbers with suits to make meaning, I recommend Alejandro Jodorowsky's *The Way of Tarot* or Camelia Elias's *Marseille Tarot: Toward the Art of Reading*.

To read the pips, you combine the meaning of the number with the meaning of the suit. If nine means magic, and cups are love, then the Nine of Cups may point to a love spell. The Three of Swords may mean a conflict is growing and spreading, while the Ace of Wands signals the start of a new creative endeavor. Like the letters of a word, each card's meaning will change depending on the cards surrounding it. Does the Ten of Coins mean a full piggy bank, or a debt coming due? You can't decide in advance. You have to see how the cards fall.

After I learned the system, a marvelous thing happened. The 1JJ began to speak to me. I asked it questions, and for the first time, I got real answers. My mother and I had both tried to read the cards in this little deck, but in the forty years since it had been printed, neither of us had ever been able to understand what they said. Forty years is an awfully long time to go without anyone understanding you, and I'm glad I was able to finally learn the 1JJ's language.

These days, I mostly use the Smith-Waite for readings, but of course I still have my 1JJ. When I do read with it, it speaks to me. I plan to pass it on to one of my daughters, if either of them wants it. Who knows? Maybe the daughter who takes it will pass it on to her daughter. Maybe it'll last a few generations before the cardstock disintegrates. Maybe some family lore will coalesce around it. Maybe the deck's origins will be forgotten completely and a legend will take their place.

But that won't change the fact that it was published by a playing card company, popularized by a Wall Street businessman, and purchased for a few bucks in 1970 by a young woman going through a hippie phase. Like the '90s resurgence of Wicca, the rise of tarot in the US is fueled just as much by capitalism as it is by spirituality.

But it doesn't matter where our tools come from. What matters is how we use them. The art of witchcraft relies on cultivating the numinous within the profane.

Besides, there's always a hidden history. The artists hunched over their engravings, the readers and cunning folk searching for messages in the cards, the folk practices few historians deemed worthy of recording. What kind of person was my mother, when she wandered Greenwich Village in bell bottoms and peasant blouses? What kind of questions did she ask the cards, and what answers did they try to give her? I think about those questions, the secret stories lost to time, and I find a humble sanctity within them.

## A Spell to Become a Seer

Start when you're wearing all the layers of yourself: every layer of your troubled history, every wrong lesson you've learned. Don't stress too much about the timing here. Look, you're wearing all those layers right now.

To become a seer, you'll need to take all those layers off. For fun, why not try to shake yourself out of all of them at once? Go on, try it. It seems like it should be so easy—just wriggle out like a snake shedding its skin. But you'll soon find out that shortcuts won't work. The only way to do this is carefully, thoughtfully, one layer at a time.

So start with the outermost layer: the heavy coat that shields you. Let's say it's your cynicism, the part of you that doesn't believe in prophecy. (Maybe a different layer is on top. That's fine. Your layers will tell you what they are, even if you have to interrogate them a bit.) Gently peel off your cynicism. Oh, look! Someone gave you this coat as a gift, didn't they? Who gave you that cynicism? They were probably looking out for you, trying to protect you from a world that preys on gullibility, but this coat is heavier than it's worth.

Once that layer is folded up and set aside, get to work on the next layer. Maybe this one is your credulity, the part of you that wants to believe in magic. It's good to have an open mind! It's good to seek out enchantment! But a true seer doesn't grasp at any old prophecy that comes along. You'll want to set this layer aside, too.

What's the next layer? Maybe it's the part of you that doubts true visions could ever come to you. But take that layer off, too. Clear sight and wisdom are your birthrights. Set aside your doubt.

What's under that? Maybe it's your ego. This layer is flashy! Wouldn't it be lovely to be a famous seer? Wouldn't it be great to be adored, sought after, and admired? Wouldn't it be nice to throw down the cards and be right every single time? But that's not how prophecy works. Set that flashy layer aside, as pretty as it is. (Don't worry, someday you can sew it into something new.)

What's the next layer under that? What's keeping you from being a seer? Maybe you only have a few layers to peel off; maybe you have a thousand. It may take just a few minutes to go through them, a quick spring cleaning of your psyche. It may take a year. I'm sorry to report this, but it could take a lifetime. Don't rush through it. A seer doesn't rush.

What's underneath all those layers? You may find that it's your childhood self, the little person who loved to play and saw stories everywhere they went. The world wants to play with you. The world wants to tell you its stories. The world wants to be your co-conspirator.

Pick up your cards, step off a cliff, and go witness the countless stories around you.

# 4

## Morrigan, Queen of the Witches

### On becoming a sacred warrior

I was lonely as a new mother, so I started looking for other witches. I found a local branch of Reclaiming, an activist, liberation-minded tradition cofounded by Starkhawk, and I started taking classes with them. One class focused on the Iron Pentacle,[2] a meditation from the Feri tradition of witchcraft that maps the concepts of sex, pride, self, power, and passion onto the body. By moving the pentacle through your body, you find and work on areas that could use more strength. Power, for instance. If, like me, you tend to see yourself as a perpetual victim pursued by omniscient boogeymen, then you may find your power point to be a bit saggy. The problem isn't the boogeymen—it's you.

---

2. For more on the Iron Pentacle, see *Ecstatic Witchcraft* by T. Thorn Coyle; *The Spiral Dance* by Starhawk; or *Magic of the Iron Pentacle* by Jane Meredith and Fio Gede Parma.

The Iron Pentacle class took place over five nights, each a week apart. On the night we were slated to study power, I arrived early and spent a few minutes wandering the shop that hosted the class. I found a thick purple candle, the kind you slide into a novena jar, and suddenly craved it. *Purple for power*, I thought, cradling the candle in my hands, forgetting that power was the theme of the evening's class. I took it upstairs to the classroom, where I found out we'd be invoking the Morrigan.

At the time, I had only the vaguest idea of who the Morrigan was. I knew she was an Irish goddess of war and fertility. Those two concepts may seem like a strange pairing until you learn, as I did that night, that the Morrigan is a goddess of sovereignty: the deity who grants someone authority and autonomy on a given swath of land, to both tend it and protect it. The teachers called her into the circle and then led us in a guided meditation in which we were wounded warriors on a battlefield. An old woman with wild gray hair and one eye poured milk over my wounds, and when I started to apologize for being such a bother, she snapped at me. "What are they teaching you in schools these days?!" she said. "You insult your body by apologizing for it!" When I thanked her, she brushed it off. "Become your power," she said. "That will be my thanks."

Later, I saw an illustration of that exact one-eyed woman in Sorita D'Este's The Guises of the Morrigan.

After that night, the Morrigan started following me around. She followed my classmates, too. I started seeing her on the internet, on blogs and message boards and online devotionals. I was puzzled, though. Back in the '90s, when I'd inhaled all those books on goddesses and paganism, the Morrigan had only ever hovered in the background. Authors mentioned her only in passing, when they mentioned her at all. It was odd that a goddess so rich with archetypal and magical significance, with so many facets and layers, with qualities that made her a natural ally for the witchcraft revival, stayed relatively dormant until the 21st century.

Isn't that interesting? Global capitalism soars to new heights of oppression and destruction, the effects of climate change kick into high gear, and a goddess of sovereignty appears on the scene?

Growing up, I was plagued by night terrors and nightmares. In preschool, I once dreamed that I walked into my parents' bedroom, and a robber with a sword leapt out of their laundry hamper. In another dream, I heard ominous drumming outside the house, and, when I peeked out from under my covers to look, a man was sitting in my window. I dreamed of horses cut in half by derailed trains, people screaming as their heads exploded, hordes of venomous animals leaping out from under the blanket. I dreamed, once, of a summer camp where the counselors were screening a filmstrip of mutilated bodies, and when I walked out of the auditorium, a woman came up to show me that she had replaced her eyes with doll eyes.

My dad's house was a common setting for my nightmares. I dreamed that I looked out of his living room window and saw a woman getting stabbed. I stared, frozen, terrified that if I moved, the killer would spot me and break in. I dreamed that a nuclear bomb was on its way, and a large diagram in the sky outside my dad's dining-room window showed where it would hit. In that huge house where my dad lived alone, I dreamed that the police were coming to get us, that the sun had gone out forever.

As scary as those dreams were, though, the night terrors were even worse. On those nights, adrenaline flooded my sleeping body and I waded helplessly through my own subconscious, speechless with brain-scrambling panic. In the worst one, my father's house was filled with monsters that looked like Jackson Pollock paintings come to life, squirming and flailing as they tore their victims apart. I wandered the halls in absolute silence, weeping and looking desperately for help, only to find one of the monsters in my father's bed.

I didn't just suffer from nightmares—I was afraid of waking life, too. I was afraid of the dark, of course. Scary movies, obviously. Once, in a video store, I saw a clip of *The Hand*, a movie about a severed hand that goes on a killing spree. I slept with my head under the covers for weeks. I was afraid of aliens abducting me, or ghosts appearing, or my house detaching from its foundation and flying into space. Eventually, the fear got so bad that I couldn't be in a room by myself, even in daylight. If I needed something from my bedroom on the most cheerful sunny afternoon, I'd bolt in and out as if I were darting into Hell. There was an ever-present terror wafting around me, an unnamed evil I was certain would grab me. They say children of divorce suffer from attachment issues, and I guess that explains part of it. All I know for sure is that I was afraid.

Most people know of the Morrigan as a goddess of warfare. In Irish mythology, she's the battle raven Badb, the prophetess and sorceress who goads armies into war, aids them with her magic, and announces the victor at the battle's end. She's also known as the Great Queen, a goddess whose power rivals the mother goddess Danu (with whom she's sometimes conflated). There's another aspect to the Morrigan, though, which scholars have unearthed through the etymology of her name. The mor in Morrigan is a cognate to the Anglo-Saxon maere, which survives in modern English in the word *nightmare*. Maere and its Germanic counterpart, *mara*, refer to fearsome female spirits. Based on this root word, scholars have suggested that Morrigan can be translated as the "Nightmare Queen" or the "Phantom Queen." Indeed, Morigain is one Irish gloss for the child-killing demon Lamia, which in turn is a gloss for Lilith.

One of my favorite manifestations of the Morrigan is in Táin Bó Regamna, in which she meets the warrior Cú Chulainn on the road shortly before a battle. Here's how Bernard Kelly describes the encounter in his retelling of the Ulster Cycle, Cúchulainn and the Crow Queen:

> He had not traveled long when he saw a strange sight coming towards him. A one-legged horse was pulling a chariot, its pole passing through the body of the beast, the point piercing the halter on its head. Within the chariot, there sat a fierce-looking woman of middle years, with a cloak of raven feathers around her shoulders and a crown of crow claws upon her head. Beside the chariot there walked a giant of a man driving a cow before him, a staff of hazelwood in his hand.

There's often a fine line between the comical and the terrifying. The Morrigan's horse, with its single leg, may sound funny on paper, but imagine seeing a beast impaled by the chariot it's pulling! The encounter marks the Morrigan as an otherworldly being, unhindered by the laws of the waking world, and that's what makes her so frightening. The horse with the chariot pole passing through its body is exactly the kind of image that pops up in nightmares.

Maybe that's why I felt such an immediate kinship with the Morrigan. Maybe she'd been visiting me all my life.

I became a Morrigan devotee. As I studied her, though, I struggled to figure out what my relationship to her was supposed to be. The Morrigan is a shape-shifter. She's three (or four or five or more) goddesses in one. As Macha, she's associated with horses and childbirth. As Nemain, she emits a scream that can kill. I started reading blogs by her followers, and they stressed that she was a battle goddess, a war goddess, a dangerous taskmaster. Only the bravest and shrewdest practitioners could work with her. If you detect some humblebragging in proclamations like those, you're not imagining it.

If all that was true, though, why did I feel her so strongly in the landscape? I had a little container garden on the roof of my apartment building, a few pots with sun-scorched zucchini and jasmine, and I felt her in the twining of the jasmine's vines and the spiders spinning webs along the pots. My job was next to a tiny nature preserve, and I felt her in the thirsty creek bed and a column of ants marching along an oak branch. I felt her in one of the autumn gales that rock Southern California, and a meteorite that I once saw sail over the horizon, and the swaying branches of the jacaranda trees. For me, the Morrigan was the breath of the wild world buried under a bloated civilization.

One of the Morrigan's aspects is Anu or Ana, the goddess of wealth and fertility. As Irish studies scholar Rosalind Clark writes in "Aspects of the Morrígan in Early Irish Literature":

> Although the juxtaposition [of destructive aspects with more nurturing ones] seems strange, there is logic in it. Because the

goddess is to preserve the *tuath,* she must be able to protect it in war as well as to provide it with the fruits of the earth, and increase both its cattle and people. The Morrigan's fertility aspect is shown in two ways—first, in her connection with cattle, and second, in her sexual prowess.

Celtic lore contains references to kings symbolically having sex with the land, binding them to the territory they rule. We see this rite echoed in a myth in which the Morrigan has sex with the Dagda, the god of plenty, in order to grant him victory in battle. This act demonstrates that sovereignty isn't just walking onto a patch of earth and announcing that you're the boss. Instead, true sovereignty—deep and sustainable sovereignty—stems from partnership with a landscape that you treat with deference and respect. According to the Santa Ynez Band of Chumash Indians, "Sovereignty is not possession of the land or control over it. Simply put, sovereignty is the living relationship between the people and the land they live on."[3]

The problem with this aspect of the Morrigan is that, nowadays, people tend to see "Earth goddesses" as fluffy, passive, and gentle. By "people," I mean people who don't have much practical experience with nature. Live through one natural disaster and you'll never see the Earth as passive again. Rather, you'll see that the goddess guards all our deaths. The 1994 Northridge Earthquake rattled my home

---

3. The quote by the Santa Ynez Band of Chumash Indians could originally be found at *chumash.gov,* but the tribe has since changed the wording of its sovereignty statement. A similar statement by the Tulalip Tribes can be found at tulaliptribes-nsn.gov.

sixty miles away in Orange County; a tornado tore through Iowa City while I sheltered with my classmates in a basement hallway; I'm currently living through a megadrought that brings wildfires. I've watched countless plants collapse under the sun or succumb to an onslaught of aphids. I've found mushrooms sprouting from animal corpses. How could I ever see nature as "fluffy"?

The Morrigan stories, especially those in the Ulster Cycle, depict a culture in which wars were fought over cattle. However, like any other myth, they retain their relevance and meaning to modern audiences through continual reinterpretation. Rather than let our readings calcify into fundamentalism, we can ask: How is my own society reflected in this myth? Do its characters experience the same struggles that my people do today? How is this story speaking across time to my culture, and what lessons or warnings does it hold?

The Ulster Cycle, for example, takes on an interesting dimension when we read it in the context of climate change. In this collection of stories, Cú Chulainn has several encounters with the Morrigan in which she offers him partnership, but he spurns her. In one encounter, in the *Táin Bó Cúaligne*, she appears as a beautiful woman and offers him love and treasures. After he rejects her offer, she tells him that she'll attack him during battle, in the guises of a wolf, an eel, and a cow. She makes good on her threat, but Cú Chulainn wounds her each time she attacks, hitting the cow in the leg, the eel in the ribs, and the wolf in the eye.

Later, Cú Chulainn comes upon an old woman milking a cow with three teats by the side of the road. The woman offers him milk, and with each drink, he blesses her, healing the wounds on her body:

her leg, her ribs, and her eye. When he realizes that the Morrigan has tricked him into healing her, he's angry, but the deed is done.

The story portrays Cú Chulainn and the Morrigan as adversaries, with the Morrigan acting as his tutelary goddess, but isn't there something about the story that feels familiar? The land offers itself to Cú Chulainn in a spirit of camaraderie; he rejects it under the misapprehension that he needs no such partnership; and the land subsequently hinders his efforts—not necessarily out of spite, but as an effect of natural law. In tricking Cú Chulainn into healing the Morrigan's wounds, the land attempts to bring him back into that mutually beneficial partnership, although Cú Chulainn is still too pigheaded to see the benefit.

That's certainly not the only way to interpret that myth, but it's an interpretation that makes sense to me as I watch industrial capitalism shred and devour the land around me. The destruction of our habitable ecosystems is happening at all levels, from the carbon cooking the atmosphere to the neighbor who carpets their yard in artificial grass. Our survival depends on a respectful partnership with nature. Why do we think lashing out at her is going to go well for us?

I see climate change happening outside my window, and I ponder the concept of sovereignty. Humans are creatures of Earth, utterly dependent on the health of the land, and we see across the globe that the oppression of people and the devastation of the environment stem from the same hubris and greed. Children mine for raw materials that end up in landfills. Entire populations are displaced by rising sea levels. Unthinkable atrocities are committed over the seductive promise of more and more wealth. I'm not the first person to wonder if, in this age of mass, mechanized violence, the Morrigan isn't gathering an army.

After I became a Morrigan devotee, I started doing what I called "fear work." All that childhood fear, my terror of solitude and the dark, my conviction that the walls teemed with monsters—I finally began to face it. Jack Kornfield writes about a Buddhist practice in which monks spend a night in the forest, sitting with their fear of tigers and other predators, and I modeled my practice on that. In a dark room, lit only by a candle on my altar, I would stare into a mirror as I chanted prayers to the Great Queen. In the dark, my face would morph into something resembling a skull. The first time it happened, I leapt away and dove for the light switch. But gradually, I learned to keep breathing when the terror rushed in, and its intensity began to ebb. One night, when my husband was out of town and I was alone in bed, I found myself pondering scary things that could grab me in the dark. I realized that I wasn't afraid. If the scary things were going to grab me, I realized, they would have done it years ago.

Later, I noticed a funny side effect of my fear work: I became a horror fan. Folk horror, to be precise. I'd sworn off horror many years before, after *The Ring* kept me up at night, but I started to feel an itch. I was hungry for the terrible awe that a good horror movie instills in you—that feeling that the reality you know could be ripped away at any moment. An elevator gushes blood; an alien bursts from your crewmate's chest; your mother saws her own head off. One day I came across a meme on Twitter, stark white text on a black background. "If you're reading this, you've been in a coma for almost 20 years," it said. "We're trying a new technique. We don't know where this message will end up in your dream, but we hope we're getting through. Please wake up." I shivered, startled, afraid that my life would suddenly dissolve around me. I still don't love jump scares, but that uncanniness is chilling and delicious, like feeling a phantom breathe on my neck.

The witch of folklore is a chthonic and liminal creature, emerging from shadow and soil, straddling this world and the Otherworld. Horror is a distillation of the vast, primordial forces we can't control: ancient predators, volatile environments, frightening urges within our own brains. The Morrigan, as sorceress and Fairy Queen, encompasses all these ideas. There's a graphic novel series, The Wicked + The Divine, in which gods incarnate on Earth in the bodies of young people and become pop stars. In the series, the Morrigan is an underground performance artist. I mean literally. To see her show, fans have to sneak into abandoned stops in the London Underground. Darkness is dangerous, yes, but it offers beauty and wisdom. It's a realm that any spiritual seeker has to explore eventually.

Maybe my intense fear of the dark, growing up, was a shield against my own power. I don't mean that in a self-aggrandizing way. I mean it in an average human way.

There's also the matter of warriorhood, because some Morrigan devotees call themselves warriors, and there are countless flavors of fear that keep us from fighting the battles we need to fight.

When I studied Buddhism, I learned about the concept of the spiritual warrior. In Shambhala: The Sacred Path of the Warrior, Chongyam Trungpa writes that the spiritual warrior recognizes that "aggression is the source of our problems, not the solution," and that fearlessness starts with confronting your own psyche. The warrior can only be of service to the world once they're armed with courageous and unflinching self-reflection. "We must try to think how we can help this world," Trungpa continues. "If we don't help, nobody will. It is our turn to help the world." Although he himself is Buddhist, Trungpa locates the idea of the spiritual warrior in myths and faith traditions all over the world, including Celtic and British lore.

Aggression is a tricky thing. It's as much a human instinct as affection is, and no reasonable person will argue that violence is always avoidable. As I write this, there are more bloody conflicts around the world, more dead children and weeping survivors, than any one person can comprehend. Yet I've met Morrigan devotees who don't seem to see their work with the goddess as a way to sanctify their acts of service, or as a way to meditate on violence as part of the human condition. Rather, they treat the Morrigan as a permission slip to behave as aggressively as they want. Aggression can feel very good in the moment, and picking a fight is much easier than exploring the root causes of anger, fear, and despair.

But to go back to the idea of sovereignty—no one is free until everyone is free. Yes, even oppressors and bullies. Any activist worth their salt will tell you that we can't just flip the hierarchies of oppression, with the formerly oppressed now able to violently oppress others. We have to dismantle those hierarchies. That's not some abstract philosophical concept. It's the only real path forward.

"Witchcraft is a tool against oppressors," writes Jason Thomas-Pitzl, in "Witchcraft Today—Witchcraft Tomorrow: A Manifesto."[4] "It

---

4. Unfortunately, it looks like Thomas-Pitzl's essay is no longer available online, although it was when I wrote the original version of this chapter. I say this as a librarian: If you want media that lasts, print is the way to go.

sides with the oppressors at its own peril, for power is ever fickle, and our gifts ever mistrusted by the bullies and abusers who would make our power their own."

To many practitioners, witchcraft is becoming synonymous with warriorhood, as a way of wresting back stolen power. How can it not? How can we practice plant magic and herbalism when our plants are drenched in pesticides and ripped out by the roots? How can we call ourselves animists, espousing belief in a universe that's awake and aware, while we let other human beings suffer? To quote the Charge of the Goddess, which many witches consider our preeminent sacred text, how can we "sing, feast, dance, make music and love" without addressing the fossil fuels that got us to our secret meeting places? At this juncture of history, to be a witch is to be a warrior. Diana and Aradia and Hekate are commonly known as queens of the witches, but now, by necessity, the Morrigan is taking her place alongside them.

I used to be a better activist than I am now. I staffed phone banks, I marched, I helped revive a dormant union at my job. Now, the moment I finish work for the day, I take care of the kids until I fall asleep. If I'm lucky I get a little writing done. I keep telling myself that fallow periods are okay, as long as I do what I can, as long as we cultivate a vision of witchcraft that sides with the disenfranchised and strives to restore a healthy relationship with the land. We can journey courageously into the dark and fearful places. We can drink from them, learn from them, use them in our sorcery. The dark is a place where reality can be ripped away, but sometimes the new reality is better than the last, even if it's frightening. In the dark, the witch can be the hunter instead of the prey.

There's one more aspect to the Ulster Cycle story I talked about earlier. When Cú Chulainn meets the Morrigan on the road, she introduces herself as a poet. Going back to Kelly's retelling: "I am a female satirist," she says. "The one who speaks the lies that tell the truth; she who has the wit and wail and wonder of the world." What is witchcraft, if not speaking a new reality into being? Who is the witch, if not someone who learns to fortify themselves with their own inherent power, and then shape the world into something better?

Here's something that many spiritual seekers don't want to hear: Most magical and spiritual work doesn't call for fancy props and costumes. It involves listening to your deepest self and doing what needs to be done. To be a witch, you have to be the most humble kind of warrior. Seek out the battles that aren't glamorous, the ones that don't stoke a fragile ego. Don't be afraid of the Nightmare Queen. After all, with climate change boiling us alive and White supremacy raging unchecked, we're already living in a nightmare.

The Goddess in all her guises has offered us her love a thousand times over. She's offered us a path back to our own strength. She offers it insistently, patiently, continuously, through the cycles of history. Now it's our job to bless her in return, accept her gifts, and heal her.

## A Spell to Become a Warrior

First, you'll need a shield of iron.

Go to the place where you feel like your truest self—the place where no one demands that you mask or change or hide any part of you. It may be the most beautiful place you know. It may be the ugliest. It's funny how these things work out sometimes. But your body will tell you that you're in the right place. Your spine will straighten, your chin will rise, and you'll unfold like a love letter.

Notice that there's a pulsing point in the crown of your head. This is the seat of your creativity, your love of making things, your craving for sensuality and pleasure. Maybe it's bright and strong; maybe it's dim and weak. It's okay. Name this point "Sex," and let it fizz for a minute or two. When you're ready, send its energy down your body to your right foot. (If, like me, you're on the asexual spectrum and you find it hard to engage with a point named "sex," feel free to name it something else. "Pleasure" could work.)

That energy will meet up with another pulse point. This point is the seat of your pride: pride in your accomplishments, pride in your heritage, pride in the mark you've made on the world. Is it overflowing, or does it feel drained? Is it healthy and right-sized, or is there something off? Name this point "Pride," gather its energy, and send it up to your left hand.

This pulse point is the seat of your self, the point that knows who you are and what your purpose is. It's the point that answers to *you, your* path, and *your* moral compass—no one else's. This is the point that's brightest when you're able to be your most authentic self. Name this point "Self," gather its energy, and send it across your body to your right hand.

This point is your point of Power. It's the point that holds your ability to exert healthy power—to stand up for yourself and others, to carve out a right-sized space in the world. It's easy to feel powerless these days. If you send your awareness to your right hand and feel your energy swallowed up by a void, you have some work to do to reclaim your power. But do your best. Name this point "Power," gather its energy, and send it down to your left foot.

This last point is the seat of everything that lights your heart on fire. It's what makes you sing, laugh, weep, and rage. It's what inspires you to create, to learn, to explore the world around you. Name it "Passion," take a minute to feel it, and then send its energy back up to the crown of your head.

Sex, Pride, Self, Power, Passion. Let this energy circulate as a five-pointed star through your body. Notice the points that are dim and tired, as if their energy has been stolen, and the ones that shine brightly. Notice the points that feel out of balance, either too small or too large.

You may not feel the Iron Pentacle turn into a shield until you've performed it a thousand and one times. That's okay. This shield doesn't have to be impenetrable. It doesn't have to fend off an army. It just has to fortify your spirit.

I could lead you on a whole separate journey to discover the injustice you're called to fight, but you already know what it is. Look, it's right in front of you. Your shield doubles as a lens, making the suffering of others sharper, clearer, impossible to ignore. There are forces hard at work stealing power that's not theirs, quashing senses of pride and self, dimming the joy of pleasure and passion.

So run your Iron Pentacle, fortify your strength, and go serve the world.

# 5

## Rainreturn

### On climate change, wildfires, and praying for rain

Things hadn't worked out at my last job, but now I was somewhere new. I was at a quieter library, a branch with a better reputation in a nicer neighborhood. No glaring problems yet. No one sexually harassing me at the reference desk, no one getting into fistfights over the public computers, no books unexpectedly covered in urine. Maybe this was the job I would keep. Maybe this was where I'd finally enjoy being a librarian. It was October, my favorite month, and I could see the loveliest hills in Los Angeles from the library's front door. Thanks to the latitude and cloudless sky of Southern California, the sun tends to be blinding most of the time in fall and winter, but when that autumn light hits those hills, they glow. I walked outside one day on my lunch break and smelled something sharp and familiar. "It smells like fall!" I thought.

Then I realized what the smell was. The Saddleridge Fire was burning a few miles away. I wasn't smelling the cozy wood smoke of fireplaces, but the ashes of plants, animals, and people's homes. I recognized the smell from the Woolsey Fire the year before, and the Skirball Fire the year before that.

The smell of fall, I realized, had become the smell of wildfires. This was what my home had become. Fall came around and the fires began; winter approached and the land burned.

Starhawk's novel *The Fifth Sacred Thing* portrays a pagan utopia: The residents of the California Bay Area have organized their society around the principles of nonviolence and the cycles of nature. The novel takes place in a future that, when the book was written, was meant to feel apocalyptic, but now it comes across as horrifically banal. In the novel, most of California is brown and desiccated, besieged by constant drought. The land is so dry that when one character gets her period, there's no water to clean herself with, and she goes days trying to ignore the dried blood on her legs.

But the grim environment of the book is mitigated by the rainy season, which commences every fall with an exuberant downpour. When the first rain of the season begins, everyone in the book erupts in celebration. Starhawk writes:

> Up and down the pathways, doors were opening and people were running out to dance deliriously. Children dashed about with pots and bowls to catch the first rainwater. Next door, the Sisters knelt in the mud to give the prayer of thanksgiving. . . . Fireworks exploded and rained down in colors that mingled bright fire

with the drops. Soon everyone's hair and clothes were damp and streaming, but they only laughed. The rain had come, even a bit early this year, and they welcomed it in the hope that it would return again and again through the winter, turning the brown hills green, filling the cisterns and replenishing the aquifers, feeding the life in the gardens and the fields that fed the people.

Starhawk calls the event "Rainreturn," and even if real Californians don't dance in the streets when it comes, it's a very real event. Throughout California's ecological history, the winter rains have kept summer and fall fires in check. In fact, fire—when it's balanced by rain—is an integral part of California's ecosystems. Small wildfires clear out dry brush so that it doesn't accumulate into fuel for larger fires. Pyriscent plants, or plants whose seeds need fire in order to germinate, are dependent on the fire cycle, as are animals that take advantage of its aftereffects for food and shelter. California Native peoples practiced fire management for thousands of years before colonists forced them to stop; according to M. Kat Andersen's *Tending the Wild*, their controlled burns increased the fertility of the land for both people and animals and helped them grow all sorts of crops.

But this fire needs water to balance it out.

The yearly dance of fire and water, water and fire, is part of what makes this land so distinctive. Watching for Rainreturn each fall ties us to its rhythms and changes, its struggles and celebrations. Most of Southern California's tap water comes from the Sierras and the Colorado River, and because this arrangement gives us the illusion of a never-ending supply of water, most of my neighbors hate the rain. I like to think, though, that each year, all over the region, gardeners and conservationists and animals and plants welcome the drenching of the land with gratitude and relief.

Now, though, that balance is off. Thanks to climate change, the rains come later and later. The conventional wisdom among native-plant gardeners is that you plant after Halloween, but now temperatures in November can reach the eighties and the rains may not come until Christmas. Plant life, already dormant from the summer heat, becomes even drier. The hot and staticky Santa Ana winds barrel in from the east. They exacerbate the fires caused by decrepit power lines and careless humans, and wildfires flare into infernos. As climate change worsens, the temperatures soar to triple digits under heat domes, and our wildflowers and redwoods wither. California, long known as a paradise, is slowly dying.

The Woolsey Fire broke my heart because it burned one of the most sacred places I know, the beach where the girls in *The Craft* filmed their seaside ritual. When I was five months' pregnant with my second daughter, I helped lead a Beltane ritual with Reclaiming in the hills above that beach. A gentle rain began to fall while I stood in the circle and invoked Inanna with one of my sister witches. I'll never forget that rain, the cool drops on my bare shoulders, the scattered rays of sunlight that caressed the landscape.

The Woolsey Fire ravaged that land, leaving it blackened and dead.

It's recovering. Some plants survived. When I was there last, I stroked their leaves and admired the flowers. I forced myself to hold two truths at once: that the surviving plants are miracles, and they don't mean the land I live on will ever be the same. It's changing irrevocably, and the species that thrive now may not be able to adapt to whatever happens over the next century or so. I cherish the life I find here while I rage against the determination, by those in power, to keep slowly killing us all.

Each time I found a new library job, I thought it would be my own little Rainreturn. At my first job, at a university library, I had a fancy title with no meaningful duties attached to it. I was asked to produce reams of documentation that no one ever read. I was expected to describe library work using corporate buzzwords like "key stakeholders" and "core competencies." I loved being around books, smelling books and ordering books and recommending books and inviting authors to come talk about their books, but where I worked, you weren't supposed to admit that you liked books. You were supposed to look on books with faint disdain, as curios that were fine for unwinding before bedtime but didn't have much to offer 21st-century college students.[5] Once, a group of students from the library school, working on a class project, came to study the fiction collection I managed. They couldn't believe that a fiction collection had so many *books*. I needed to *innovate*, they explained. Yes, the collection needed to be more innovative. How so? I asked. What, e-books? Because I was working on that! I was writing a proposal to—no, the students sniffed, not *e-books*. E-books were still books, and books weren't innovative. In the end, they never really explained what they meant. Books were just an atrociously uncool thing to have sitting around in a library. Honestly, I suspect they just didn't like to read.

---

5. I should mention, here, that the first library director I worked for loved books as much as I did, but she ran screaming for the same reasons I did.

I left the university for a public library—where everyone at least agreed that books are very cool. My first post was as a teen services librarian, which was what I'd secretly wanted to do in library school all along. I started writing down ideas before the job even started, brainstorming plans for arts and crafts workshops. I looked up local high schools where I could do outreach. I jotted down titles for book displays.

My first day, I happily reported for training at the main library, after which I'd be deployed to my branch. The training started with an elderly librarian complaining about patrons who faked disabilities so that we'd have to let their dogs in, and then we went around and introduced each other.

As soon as I said the name of my branch, the trainers winced. "There are no teens at that branch," one of them said.

Another pulled up the list of police reports that had been filed there. "It's the most dangerous branch in the system," she said.

I showed up the next day and found the library surrounded by porn shops and bars. There was no way a parent with any sense would let their teen come to a place like this.

"Our job here is to *pretend* to be librarians," the children's librarian told me one day, as we surveyed the deserted children's section on a weekday afternoon. Each picture book was shelved and pristine, each toy tucked in its basket. Every teen librarian before me had transferred out of the branch as soon as they could, leaping at jobs in adult services, outreach, cataloging, any department that would take them.

The library's main clientele, I soon found out, were men who had hit rock bottom and had nowhere else to go. These men—they were mostly men—were in the throes of addiction, homelessness, and

*Witch Blood Rising*

severe mental illness, sometimes all three at once. They smoked crack on the front steps and used heroin at the computers. They relieved themselves in the stacks and the elevator. They cornered us and groped us and screamed and broke furniture when they were upset. We were told to assume that every patron was armed. Some of the library's rules were explicitly anti-homeless—no eating, no sleeping, no pets, no large bags—while others were more reasonable, like no masturbating.

We spent most of our time grimly enforcing the rules. We looked the other way whenever we could, allowing people their desperately needed naps and companion animals. Sometimes patrons wanted something we couldn't give them. "I want you to tell me the title of every screenplay you have on the shelf," one patron demanded over the phone. When I tried to explain that I didn't have hours to spend reciting titles to her, she exploded. "You lazy fucking bitch!" she screamed.

It's hard to describe just how joyless and prisonlike the atmosphere was at that little neighborhood library. We weren't allowed to leave early, and our pay was docked if we were even a minute late. I had headaches every day. I was always sick with some cold or another. Emotionally, I felt numb, but my body sounded every alarm.

Wouldn't it be lovely if this were the story of how I single-handedly turned that library branch around? But this isn't that story. Instead, it's the story of how I tried my best, burned out, and escaped. There's an aggressive edge to many miracle-worker stories: "This hero figured out how to save a thousand starving babies using only a tin can and a piece of string," the narrative goes. "If you're a good person and you put your mind to it, you can do anything you want with no help at all!"

Except you can't. Not in real life. Not even if you're a witch; not even if the Morrigan is appearing to you in meteors and streambeds.

Humans, like all things, are interdependent, and savior stories erase the massive amounts of community and resources that make change happen.

There were little moments here and there when I felt like I was actually doing something useful. The emergency shelters were always full and the day shelters had odd hours, but occasionally I was able to help a homeless visitor get a meal or a shower. Once a month another library branch held an outreach event where people could get food, haircuts, cell phones, and other necessities, and I would go there to do intake interviews and give out coffee. It felt good to give out coffee. Cup after cup after cup of coffee. "Can I get seconds?" people would ask. "Thirds?" Of course! Fourths, fifths, whatever they wanted! We always had enough coffee.

The people who hung out at my branch suffered from what Father Gregory Boyle, founder of the gang rehabilitation organization Homeboy Industries, calls a "lethal absence of hope": a despair so profound that they could no longer imagine futures for themselves. But the people who went to the outreach event were trying to scrape their lives back together. One guy came up to me and asked if there were any psychiatric services there. "I need to check myself into someplace tonight," he said. "I'm afraid I might hurt myself." Luckily, I knew who to ask. There was a retired woman in the neighborhood who spent her days serving homeless communities, hooking them up with food and clean clothes and social services. I grabbed her, and she grabbed a social worker, and they took the guy to a corner of the room. Over the next half hour, I snuck glances as they talked. He cried for a while, and then I overheard him say he was saving up for a tent. I didn't see him again after that day. Maybe that's because something terrible

*Witch Blood Rising*

happened, or maybe it's because things got better. I'll never know, so I'll always hope.

"The problem, of course, with throwing people away," Octavia E. Butler wrote in *Parable of the Talents*, "is that they don't go away. They stay in the society that turned its back on them. And whether that society likes it or not, they find all sorts of things to do." As I write this, the average home in Los Angeles now costs over a million dollars, yet the richest people in the city keep blocking the construction of affordable housing. The ruling class is playing a game of chicken to see how long they can ignore the housing crisis before it engulfs them. They're playing the same game with the wildfires. Every year megawealthy places like Brentwood and Malibu burn, so the rich hire private firefighters—yes, that's actually a thing!—and collect insurance payouts.

The wildfires, it must be noted, are directly tied to the housing crisis. When developers can't build housing in the city, they do it in the land surrounding the city, pushing the electrical grid farther and farther out into wildlands, where poorly maintained power lines ignite poorly managed forests. Everything burns and everyone loses.

In 2019, when I wrote the essay that would become this chapter, the Kincade and Getty Fires broke out. As I revised it, the Tick and Easy Fires broke out. The day I finished it, I saw a plume of smoke over Griffith Park, home of the Hollywood sign and the famous mountain lion P-22. A year after that essay was first published, the suburb of Altadena burned, and the sun over the city turned blood-red in an angry brown sky. There are too many fires to keep track of these days, one after another after another.

My husband's family lives in Northern California, and some of them work on farms. He's been a staunch atheist as long as I've known him, but on the first day of the Kincade Fire, which burned almost 78,000 acres in Sonoma County, he asked if we could do a protection ritual for his sister. I'm cagey about sharing my witchcraft with others, even those closest to me. Witchcraft is sacred because it's secret. I like to hold it close and protect it. But when someone asks me for help with magic, I never say no.

We put the kids to bed, and I led him through a brief spell that involved dousing a candle in water. My sister-in-law's farm survived the fire more or less intact.

The other farm, though, one belonging to my husband's aunt and uncle, met a different fate. I'd visited that farm many times. Once, I had gone for a walk by myself and sat in a quiet corner of the property. I felt frustrated that only the wealthy could afford to own land this beautiful, that I would likely never be able to live here myself, that it was impossible to live in my country without occupying stolen land in the first place. Imagine the workings I could do if I lived out here, I mused, feeling like half a witch. Imagine the herbs I could grow, the plants I could study, the spirits I could meet. At home in the city, my container garden was wilting under yet another heat wave. I'd never had a real garden in the ground, never in my entire adult life.

As I sat there feeling jealous, I also took in the peace of the woods, the mottled greens of the mosses and lichens on the oak trees, the innumerable ghosts who whispered and sighed in the wind. Around me there were wildflowers that I usually only saw in books. As I sat, a deer with two fawns ambled down the path and disappeared around a bend. My husband's aunt had decorated her barn with antlers and snakeskins. Unlike the suburbs I'd grown up in and the apartment building I lived in now, this land visibly bristled with life.

After the fire, my husband's family sent word: All of it was gone, burned, destroyed.

Rainreturn used to feel like a covenant. *Hold on for just a few more weeks*, the rain used to say, as the land crisped, as staticky doorknobs started to zap your fingers and the air grew so dry it made your nose bleed. *I'm coming*, the rain would say. *Don't worry, I'm coming.* Rainreturn was always a promise renewed, a loving parent calling hello.

Now, though, Rainreturn can feel like an opiate. Each year, the rains come later and later, their payloads smaller and smaller. But when the rains do return, the wildfires go out and the hills turn green. We pretend we still live in the same California in which we grew up, and nothing is done to address next year's fires. Even I find myself infected by false hope. I decide—*I decide!*—that surely we'll find the grand unified solution to climate change soon, and the revolution will be easy and bloodless, and I'll somehow end up with a lush, sprawling herb garden outside a cozy little house. Part of me forgets that the land as I know it is dying. Even the most pragmatic part of me can't quite comprehend the sheer scale of destruction that's happening, the fearsome transformation that's occurring. At Rainreturn, the emotional part of me refuses to see it.

And really, like Cú Chulainn ignoring the signs that the woman he's antagonizing is a goddess, all these problems stem from a refusal to really look at something and recognize it. The higher-ups at my job refused to see that they were failing both community members and employees. Wealthy Angelenos refuse to see that simply blocking new housing doesn't preserve their luxurious way of life; it just creates tent cities at their doorsteps. Everyone searches for the little respites—a successful homeless outreach event, a green hill in February—that allow them to forget the looming disaster. We gawk at the wildfires, year after year, and pretend we don't see the very obvious pattern.

Witches are often accused of escapism, playing dress-up and claiming self-aggrandizing magic powers. Yes, too many witches choose fantasy over reality. But the true witch has always been an oracle. As seers, our job is literally to see. We see probable outcomes through divination. We see the fractures in our communities from our vantage points on the fringe. We see the medicine in plants, and the harmony of the stars and planets, and the denizens of the spirit world screaming at us to take action.

What if we bring forth a massive Rainreturn, a deluge that washes away the corruption and gluttony that allowed all this to happen? What if we whip up a storm that dissolves all the brutality that industrial capitalism has nurtured? What if our Rainreturn washes our eyes clean and allows us to see our ecosystems, our myriad human and nonhuman neighbors, as the sacred beings that they are?

What if? If something as unthinkable as climate change is possible, then its antidote must be, too.

I said that my husband's family's farm was completely destroyed, but we later found out that wasn't entirely true. It turns out there was a single crate of chicks that was left behind in the evacuation. Incredibly, the chicks survived. The chicks, like the plants at the beach, force us to hold both rage and gratitude at once. A crate of trapped and helpless baby birds survived the Kincade Fire. If they can do that, we can do anything.

After six months on the job, new librarians were allowed to transfer to other branches. But when my six-month mark came, there was a problem: HR wasn't accepting transfer applications. They said they were too busy with other things. I called the union, and they confirmed that HR was breaking the contract, but the union was fighting too many other battles to take up this one, too. Meanwhile, things got worse at the branch. It developed a rat infestation, and I found droppings in my desk. I began to have trouble breathing, and a doctor gave me an inhaler.

But magic I had worked months before finally came through, albeit in kind of a pathetic way. I'd worked a spell to make sure I was out of that branch by autumn, and right around the fall equinox, I found a shingles rash on my side. I was thirty-eight years old. "What are you doing that's stressing you out so much!?" my doctor asked me, aghast. It was enough to get a doctor's note, which warranted an emergency transfer.

The new branch was better. I was a children's librarian now. I led storytimes and held LEGO days. Sometimes the kids gave me portraits they'd drawn of me. I still cried in the car on my way to work. There were still problem patrons. One man almost punched me, and another muttered "bitch ass" under his breath anytime a librarian passed him. My new branch manager periodically called surprise staff meetings so that she could run through a litany of our screwups. One of my coworkers came back from every break smelling like marijuana, and I didn't blame him.

*But things are better now,* I told myself. *This is better.*

One evening in November, I was sitting at the reference desk, waiting out the closing shift so that I could go home and kiss my sleeping children goodnight. It was a quiet night, with only a few people at the tables and computers, and the only sound was the hum of the HVAC. At home, my husband was getting ready to fly out to a job interview in Massachusetts, where housing was marginally cheaper. The thought of being able to afford a house with a yard, and keeping a real garden, filled me with a stinging want. In the end, my husband got the job, but the salary was too low for him to take it.

The library building had several skylights, and gradually I noticed a sound like pebbles rolling around on top of them. I stopped scrolling through Instagram and listened. The sound grew into a roar that I hadn't heard in months, and with my breath catching, I quickly said a little prayer of thanks. One of my coworkers was looking out the front door, and I told him I'd be right back. I went out into the darkness and saw the parking lot shiny with water, with sweeps of raindrops falling past the streetlights. I stood in it, smelling the petrichor I hadn't smelled in months, letting the water flatten my hair and dot my clothes. Who cared if I sat back down at the reference desk soaking wet? No one cared at all, and, for once, it was great.

Our land is dying; our neighbors are suffering; everything sacred is being hunted down and destroyed. But that night, I paused and felt gratitude for the rain, and even now I know it was the right thing to do.

*Witch Blood Rising*

## A Spell to Bring the Rain

You can call the rain anywhere you like, but to do your work as a witch, you'll need to find the fire first.

To search for fire, step outside your door. Go to a wild place and bring a simple offering with you—a vessel of clean water, maybe, or a small wreath of flowers—that will bring the spirits joy. One of those spirits will come to you. They may look frightening. They may look beautiful. Whatever you do, don't stare. Just ask them how to find the fire that's threatening their home, and they'll point the way, either through space or through time.

You'll need to see the fire for yourself before you can figure out how to deal with it. It might take the form of a burning habitat. It might be a smokestack belching poison. Maybe it's oil slipping through the ocean. It might take a different form altogether, so trust your inner eye on this one. Not all fires look like fires at first, and sometimes it takes that tug in your gut to recognize what you're witnessing. When you feel that tug, know that this is the fire you need to quench.

But what now? It may feel impossibly big. That's what the fire wants you to think, though. It wants you to feel small and powerless. If you succumb to the urge to slink away and do nothing, you'll know it has you under its spell.

So resist that. Fight it. Open your mouth and yell out thunder. Raise your arms and bring down torrents. Let your words blow the fire out like a candle, let your steps smother it to dying embers, let your hands pour raindrops on the burns left behind. *You are the rain:* your body, your voice, and your spirit. It really is that simple to bring water to parched land, and that difficult.

To bring the rain, you have to find the fire. And I'm so sorry to tell you, my beautiful stout-hearted witch, that there are plenty of fires to choose from.

# 6

## Thy God Loki

### On horned gods, neurodivergence, and queerness

One day, I went to my therapist fretting because I couldn't get Loki out of my head. Not the Norse god—the Marvel character. I'd been getting more and more into the Marvel Cinematic Universe, learning all the story arcs and sprawling lore in its movies and TV shows, and I'd just finished watching season 1 of *Loki*. In *Loki*, the trickster god, brother of the thunder god Thor, is swept into an alternate reality after escaping the Avengers. For the crime of breaking the timeline, Loki is arrested by a regime called the Time Variance Authority, recruited by a time cop named Mobius, and ordered to hunt down a female variant of himself named Sylvie. In the ensuing chaos, he flies through a redemption arc that transforms him from a narcissistic mass murderer into a vulnerable, contemplative hero. Some Marvel fans loved it; others hated it; I obsessed over it.

"I keep having these dreams," I said. I was embarrassed because, growing up, I'd been teased for my hyperfixations. Every so often a character would take up residence in my brain, riding around with me throughout my days. I'd pretend to be a ninja turtle in the backyard, then continue to be a ninja turtle at the dinner table, then at bedtime, and then when I woke up the next morning, and then I'd accidentally call a classmate Donatello. But I wasn't a kid anymore. I didn't want Loki hitchhiking in the back of my mind for six months. In my weirdest dream, which I had after watching Loki break down crying in episode 1, I dreamed that Thor chained him down and beat him until they began to resemble each other. Thor became deranged and villainous, Loki noble and martyred. I would make a psychiatrist appointment, I decided. I would go back on medication.

But my therapist's response surprised me. "You're the second client to come in talking about that show," she said. "The other person can't get it out of their head, either." Apparently *Loki* had managed to twang some deeply resonant string in its viewers. I hadn't expected that at all. I'd thought my mind was just doing its usual thing, shunting off in a direction no one else would understand.

After the session, I went home and tended my altar, lighting a candle and setting out some candies and kissing the roebuck skull that hung on the wall. I watched the candle flame, still mulling over Loki, and the tines of the roebuck's antlers cast flickering shadows on the wall: a pair of silently dancing horns looming over me, as always. Suddenly, though, a new presence lurked inside them.

After my grandmother died, my family and I went to clean out her apartment and I found a copy of my parents' wedding invitation. I smiled, opened it, and then did the math.

My sister saw my face. "Yeah," she said, although I hadn't asked her anything. "I saw that earlier."

The fact that she found out before me made it so much worse.

After that, the knowledge that I'd been an accident served as an easy explanation for everything that was wrong with my life. At my wedding reception, our college friends lovingly praised and roasted my husband but had nothing to say about me. At a party in grad school, one of my classmates stuck a piece of trash in the brim of my hat, and I unwittingly wore it around for two hours. After the party, seething, I thought of the invitation I'd found in my grandmother's things. Of *course* people picked on me! I was a mistake, not supposed to be here, not supposed to exist!

But there was something else going on, too. No one else, I gradually noticed, had to cover their ears when the shower turned on, or cut every tag out of their clothing. Everyone else seemed to communicate in code, through telepathy. I always said the wrong thing and got strange looks, or made jokes that no one understood. I didn't have crushes on the right people in the right ways. Trying to make friends, doing all the things I was told would help me grow close to people, always felt like putting together a puzzle. I'd put in the hours and then reach for the very last piece, only to discover that it wasn't there.

The term *neurodivergent* refers to normal variations in the human brain that are often considered disorders, and I began to realize I was neurodivergent around the same time that I finally figured out that I was queer. As Jenara Nerenberg points out in her book *Divergent*

*Mind*, the way mental health issues are compartmentalized belies the true diversity of the human mind. I'd been treated for various symptoms over the years, but discrete diagnoses like OCD and depression are often symptoms of a deeper root cause. Differences in sensory processing and attention all fall on a spectrum of human cognition, and what seems like a disorder is often only our society's failure to accommodate it. Like gender and sexuality, the makeup of the human mind is slippery, with near-infinite possibilities.

Many neurodivergent people report feeling immense relief when they finally figure out what's going on. I guess I felt some of that, but mostly I felt deflated. I would never be able to make friends. I would always be like this.

Comics are a haven for misfits, so it's no surprise that Marvel fans fell hard for Loki in the movie *Thor*. When we meet him, Loki is an outsider, part of the royal family of Asgard but hovering unhappily on the edge of Thor's friend group. No one likes him much, and he has a history of acting out. Loki's feelings of inadequacy, of being inexplicably out of sync, are explained when he finds out that he's actually a kind of primordial giant called a jotun, raised to believe he was Asgardian. Odin tells Loki that he found him as an infant, abandoned by the jotuns and left out in the cold to die. Loki's secret adoption, it turns out, was a political move intended to strengthen ties between Asgard and Jotunheim, now rendered obsolete by the breakdown of the peace treaty between the two kingdoms. Making matters infinitely worse, the Asgardians hate and demonize the jotuns. Loki finds out that, in the eyes of his people, he's literally a monster.

It's one of the better villain origin stories in the Marvel Cinematic Universe. What do you do after you find out that it's not your

imagination, that you really are unwanted, that there's an invisible difference living inside you that repulses everyone you love? How do you
manage that pain? Where do you send it? In my case, I embarked on
years of therapy. In Thor, Loki tries to kill Thor and the jotuns and
then jumps into a wormhole. Everyone has their coping strategies.

There's a poignant moment in season 1, episode 4 of Loki, based
on one of the original Norse myths, when an Asgardian named Sif
confronts him with a lock of hair he cut from her head while she was
sleeping. We don't know why he did it (although some fans speculated
that he and Sif were sleeping together). He just describes it as "a bit
of fun." Sif doesn't see it that way, though. "You deserve to be alone,
and you always will be," she hisses. It's telling that she knows exactly
which insult will hurt the most. It shows that Thor and his friends
have always known how lonely Loki was. For a couple of episodes
it looks like Sif will be proven wrong, as Loki lets his guard down
and manages to make the first real friends of his thousand-year life
in Mobius and Sylvie. But in the season finale, Sylvie shoves him into
an alternate timeline and strands him there. Season 1 ends with Loki
taking in his new surroundings—frightened, heartbroken, and com-
prehensively alone. It's a betrayal that every outcast can relate to.

One night, I got a text from a relative who'd been calling me names
for years. He liked to call me "passive" and "brainless," both of which are
particularly loaded insults when your mind often chatters too loudly
for you to hear anything else. Here's a fun fact about neurodivergent
people: We're often doing twice as much mental work as everyone else,
frantically trying to filter out all the noise and stimulation pouring in
through our senses so that we can focus on whatever task is in front
of us. Calling a neurodivergent person lazy while they're doing all that

extra work is just about the cruelest thing you can do. The text from this person wasn't anything noteworthy, but it set me off, and soon I found myself crying to my husband about that last Loki scene. I felt silly crying over a Marvel show, but damn, that last shot really got to me. "A monster who ends up alone," I said, thinking of the unrelenting patterns of bullying and fizzled relationships in my own life. "If that doesn't sound like me, then I don't know what does."

Like Hermes or Raven, the original Loki of Norse mythology is a trickster and culture bringer, inventing or securing treasures like the world's first fishing net, Odin's eight-legged horse Sleipnir, and Thor's magic hammer. But while some tricksters are revered, Loki is reviled. Snorri Sturluson, the medieval author of the *Prose Edda*, calls Loki "evil," "treacherous," and "the Disgrace of All Gods and Men." Some modern Heathens, venerating the Norse gods, refuse to even say Loki's name in ritual space. Indeed, in the myths, he's a troublemaker. Out of what seems like sheer malevolence, he shaves Sif's head and engineers the death of the beloved god Baldr. In the poem Lokasenna, he jealously kills a lauded servant at a feast and then systematically insults every god sitting at the table. Even the problems he solves for the gods tend to be problems he himself created.

Like his Marvel counterpart, Loki hangs out with the Aesir, even though he isn't one of them. We know he's a blood brother to Odin and the offspring of a taboo union between a goddess and a jotun, but there's no actual origin story. He's just there, skulking eternally around the edges of the pantheon. His gender, in particular, is constantly called into question. In one myth, he convinces Thor to dress up like Freyja, while he himself dresses as a lady in waiting. In another, he gives birth to Sleipnir by shape-shifting into a mare and getting pregnant. In yet another, which is charged with homophobic symbolism, he ties a goat to his testicles and screams in pain as it yanks him around the room, much to the delight of the gods.

The ambiguity at the heart of Loki's character hints at stories that have been lost, a depth and significance that Snorri and other storytellers left out. Some scholars believe that the Loki we've inherited is actually a composite figure. Loki may originally have been a pre-Christian trickster god who, in a culture in which masculinity wasn't inherent but rather achieved by heroic acts, occupied a low-ranking but normal space between male and female. As the Nordic countries were Christianized and gender ambiguity came to be seen as threatening and unnatural, the androgyne trickster may have been combined with a Devil figure—an association that Marvel artist Jack Kirby cemented in 1962 with the addition of the iconic golden horns.

The original context of the myths is lost, though, so we have to approach the Norse Loki through the lens of the myths we do have. Some modern witches and pagans see him as a force of change and transformation, or Odin's shadow self. Others have embraced his queerness.

Because wow, does Loki embody some delicious queerness—not just in the Norse myths, but in Marvel comics, too. In 2008, Marvel introduced Lady Loki, or Loki sporting a new female body. (The story of how she got that body is complicated, so just roll with it.) Gradually, Lady Loki grew into more than just a plot twist or a disguise, ultimately becoming as central to Loki's character as his male form. In one storyline, Odin calls Loki "my child who is both [son and daughter]." In later storylines, Loki switches gender seemingly at random, whenever he/she/they feel like it. Loki and Lady Loki are one. Loki is simply Loki.[6]

I tried she/they pronouns for a little while, but it didn't feel quite right, so I went back to she/her. I realized that if I could have any gender I wanted, Loki would be my gender. The androgyne trickster, the shape-shifter.

But how much of that desire is inherent queerness, and how much is my failure, growing up, to perform femininity the right way? I always felt too ugly to be a girl, but I think I still mostly wanted to be one. How much of my gender is queerness, and how much is neurodivergence and monstrousness, that Devil's mark showing itself? It's impossible to say.

Here's another thing I wonder about the Loki of Norse mythology. What originally happened to him to make him so violent? The Aesir are already a violent lot, punishing him for his tricks by letting dwarves sew his lips shut and having a snake drip poison into his eyes. But how did Loki get that way in the first place? What original violence, left off the page, did the Aesir commit against him, his gender fluidity, his inescapable otherness?

Snorri, after calling Loki evil and treacherous, adds that he has "the wisdom known as cunning." In one story, Loki saves himself from being beheaded by telling his executioners that while he did techni-

---

6. Odin's line about Loki as both son and daughter is in Marvel's *Original Sin #5.5*, which is included in *Loki: Agent of Asgard: The Complete Collection*. For more about gender-fluid Loki, I suggest the collected *Defenders: Beyond* by Al Ewing and Javier Rodriguez, and Al Ewing's 2023–2024 run of *Immortal Thor*.

cally promise them his head, he never told them they could touch his neck. Like other tricksters, Loki survives because his mind works differently than those around him, noticing details and making connections that others miss. In that sense, cunning isn't far removed from neurodivergence.

And then there are his horns: those lightning rods for divine wisdom, those symbols of magic and witchery. In Marvel lore, Loki's horns represent his mastery of sorcery, serving as an insignia he's earned after years of study. In antiquity, horns represented strength and sovereignty.[7] The first time he put on his Loki costume, Tom Hiddleston remarked on how "enormously powerful" wearing the horns made him feel.[8] And he does look powerful—like a serpent, like a little dragon. I can't help but notice that, in the past few years, artists and illustrators have started putting horns on the Norse Loki. A few hundred years from now, will a horned Loki simply be canon? Will folklorists and spiritual seekers be floored when they find out that the Eddas don't actually mention any horns? What a clever trickster, using a twelve-cent comic book to slide into the ranks of the horned gods.

Perhaps, donning the horns, Loki accesses the divine logic behind what we consider disorder, and shapes reality accordingly. Those of us roaming the terrain of disorder see ourselves in Loki, in his exquisite monstrousness, and find strength and meaning in it. After all, what does cunning look like when you don't have to use it for mere survival?

---

7. For more on the meaning of horns in antiquity, see *Horns of Honor by Frederick Thomas Elsworthy.*
8. This particular Tom Hiddleston interview is hard to track down these days, but you can still occasionally find it floating around the internet.

What gifts and possibilities do we miss out on when we talk about differently built minds and bodies as broken and wrong? What if the jotun in his horned regalia—or the witch with her demonic bloodline—was never a monster at all?

At the height of my fixation, I discovered an intriguing Twitter account, @ThyGodLoki, that periodically tweeted out quips from the perspective of the Marvel character. Most of the tweets are mildly funny, like *Out of all enemies of the Avengers, I was the best looking*, or *I would never stab you in the back. True friends stab you in the front.* But one day, the account startled me by tweeting this: *You are not a burden. You are not worthless. You are not unloved.*

As a trickster, trust me when I tell you, your mind is just trying to trick you into believing those negative thoughts. But it is merely a bad illusion.

You matter so much.

The replies quickly filled with people thanking Loki, at least a couple purportedly in tears. Maybe we all love this character because we feel as broken as he does, and encouragement from him carries extra weight because he knows what we've been through. Or maybe we're struck by the idea that Loki matters—not just as a heel for the Avengers or a procurer of magic items for the Aesir, but as a being in his own right, someone who exists for the sake of his own strange perfection. In *Loki*, Loki learns that the TVA has been corralling him into villainy his whole life, tweaking and redoing every moment of his existence so that his worst acts will inspire others to become heroes. But Mobius helps him break free of the cycle. "You could be whoever, whatever you want to be. Even someone good," Mobius tells him near the end of season 1, prepared to shatter the universe to free him.

But the end of *Loki* season 2 is even more devastating than the end of season 1. Loki finds out that the timestream is controlled by a machine called the Temporal Loom. To free the infinite realities of the multiverse, Loki has to break the loom, but that destroys the timelines. To revive them, he takes them in his hands and entombs himself in Yggdrasil, the World Tree. There he sits, seemingly for all eternity, keeping the multiverse alive with his magic. "I don't want to be alone," he tearfully tells Sylvie in the penultimate episode, before ending up alone for the rest of time.

It's a horrific ending—but what makes it even worse is that no one else in the show seems to care. "It's weird that Loki's not here, isn't it?" Sylvie says to Mobius at the end. Mobius looks sad, but he doesn't have any obvious plans to rescue Loki from the tree. The message for many fans, including me, was devastating: If you're monstrous you don't get a happy ending. The best thing you can do for the people you love is go away forever.

The challenge, after an ending like that, is to remember that if Loki's worth is inherent, then mine—and yours—must be, too.

The human mind is a chimera: neocortex, limbic system, brainstem, and all the tangled histories and calculations that form what we call the "self." We are all shape-shifters, each brain a roomful of alter egos in chattering conversation. The fascination with Loki I see among Marvel fans, witches, and scholars reminds me that the world is full of outcasts, sifting through those conversations in search of something good.

Other members of the Aesir had public shrines erected to them, prayers composed in their honor. Not so with Loki, it seems. There are no physical landmarks or days of the week named after him, no unearthed temples, no evidence of a widespread cult in his name. But some scholars have speculated that, because tricksters and culture heroes tended to be honored more in private spheres, the artifacts of Loki's worship may have just been too ephemeral to survive. I don't know if that's true, but I find it a more compelling explanation than the idea that a character so beloved, so beguiling and enduring, never once enjoyed an offering or hymn.

At my altar, under my roebuck skull, I added Loki's name to the list of horned gods I venerate. I set out an offering for the trickster god, but also for my own cryptic brain. What should I ask Loki for, I wondered? For my fractured self to be as beautiful as his, I decided.

I tenderly fussed over my brooding little pantheon. The gods and spirits I love may seem like the kind of crowd any sensible person would stay the hell away from, but I felt a feral love surrounding me. On the wall, the shadows danced.

---

## A Spell to Call on the Trickster

If you feel an affinity with the Trickster, you'll want to undertake this journey as soon as you can. You don't want to end up trying to get to know the trickster at the last second. This relationship can take time to figure out, and you want to know where the two of you stand when you find yourself in a crisis.

First, take a quick trip to the realm of monsters. It's somewhere in the World Tree, but no one knows exactly where. The roots? The trunk? The highest, farthest branch? The lore doesn't say. But the Trickster has already laid out a true path for you, even if that path looks like it's leading you in exactly the wrong direction. Remember that when it comes to the Trickster, nothing is ever as it seems, but the deepest truths still shine through. Follow your feet, follow the path, and you'll reach the realm of monsters.

Just as dawn reveals things you'd never notice at night, so does the realm of monsters reveal your own monstrousness. Take a moment, when you arrive, to admire yourself. It's okay, you can admit it: You look damn good as a monster. Notice all the things about you that you're supposed to feel ashamed of. How strange and wonderful that in the light of the realm of monsters, they suddenly look so beautiful. Did I say take a moment? Maybe you should take an hour. Maybe you should take a day or a year or a century to admire the beauty of your monstrousness. Take the rest of your life.

Search the realm of monsters with your monsters' eyes, and you'll eventually find the Trickster. You may find them in a grand palace, lounging on a throne. Or maybe a crumbling little cottage. You may stumble into them on the path. There's no telling what form they'll take. But listen closely to what the Trickster tells you, because that's how they'll reveal who they are. You may have to turn away an imposter or two. Just make sure you don't snub the Trickster when they actually appear.

You don't need to give the Trickster a physical offering. You don't need to bring them a gift. Instead, they'll ask you for something even more precious: the truest lie you've ever carried with you. Maybe you'll need to sit down before you start your journey and come up with it. Maybe it'll occur to you when you stand before the Trickster. Either way, make sure you're ready to hand it over when the Trickster tells you it's time.

In return, the Trickster will grant you one boon. Take it from their hands. Hang it around your neck or slip it in your pocket. Guard it carefully. Feed it often. When you need the Trickster's help, use the boon to call on them, and they'll lend you their power. Choose your timing carefully, though, because you can only use it once.

That isn't to say that the Trickster will never help you again, of course. But that's an arrangement you'll have to work out with them another time. Don't worry—you can return to the realm of monsters whenever you want. Part of you is there right now, waiting for the rest of you to catch up.

*Witch Blood Rising*

# 7

# Athena's Loom

## On spinning and weaving
## as magical acts

### Part 1: The Elizabeth

I developed an eccentric pastime whenever things were slow at the library reference desk: I started spending hours searching for used spinning wheels on Craigslist. Most new spinning wheels cost about a thousand dollars. I didn't have a thousand dollars. Did I have room for a spinning wheel in my home? No, I didn't have that, either. But that was a problem I could deal with later. For the time being, I looked.

Most wheels that came up were a hundred years old or more—beautiful decorations for a folksy aesthetic, but not ideal for someone just starting out. One day, though, I hit the jackpot. Someone an hour's drive away was selling an Ashford Elizabeth in perfect condition for $300. I held my breath as I feverishly clicked through the photos. A patron came to the desk, and I had to swallow the urge to tell them to scram. Ashford is a well-known maker of wheels and looms, and the Elizabeth is their Saxony-style model, which means that it looks like it came out of a fairy tale. I don't want many material things in life, but this spinning wheel? Oh, I wanted this thing.

My mother first taught me to knit when I was in college. It was a spur-of-the-moment thing, born from a quiet afternoon during the holidays. She decided she wanted to relearn to knit and I went with her to the yarn store. Rows of colorful wool bundles lined the shelves, as inviting as the paints in an art supply store, and I picked out some blue and gray tweed. After her own quick refresher, my mother taught me the knit stitch. By the time I got back to school, I had made my very first scarf.

Over the years, I made Estonian lace shawls, Fair Isle hats and mittens, baby blankets, sweaters, and too many scarves to count. It didn't take long to master knitting—people never believe me when I insist that it's easier than it looks—but spinning was another matter.

I taught myself to spin on a tool called a drop spindle. The drop spindle looks like an oversized wooden top, and what it does is nothing short of magical. Attach a bit of fiber to the tip, like wool or flax, and then flick the spindle to get it spinning. Let go of it, and the spindle will hang from the fiber. Pull little bits of fiber from your supply (a process called drafting) to feed the length holding the spindle, and the spindle will twist it into yarn. Why does the fiber have to be twisted? Because the twist allows microscopic barbs to lock together, making the yarn strong and durable. Before the spindle sinks to the floor, give the yarn you've just made a quick tug to launch the spindle into the air. Catch it, wind the yarn onto the shaft, and start the process all over again.

For roughly twenty thousand years, this is how every single thread of every single textile was made. Fishing nets, togas, tunics, robes, shawls, dresses, cloaks, sails, curtains, tapestries, rugs, towels, bed sheets—everything, *everything* had to be spun by hand. The earliest evidence of fiber arts, like the needles and beads that survive where the actual thread has long since decomposed, dates back to the Upper Paleolithic. Spinning, both by individuals and in workshops, has been well documented in ancient Greece and Egypt. In her book *Women's Work*, historian Elizabeth Wayland Barber suggests that the *Venus de Milo*, before she lost her arms, was originally holding a spindle in one hand and a distaff (a rod used to hold raw fiber) in the other. Spinning is one of humanity's most ancient crafts, and because it's a craft that can be quickly put down to tend to hungry babies and other household duties, it largely fell to women.

Spinning was so time-consuming, and the thread it produced so essential, that for centuries textiles were precious enough to be used as currency. Wherever you happen to be sitting at this moment, look around and you'll probably see textiles everywhere. Take a quick count of all the cloth items around you or on your body. Now imagine all that thread being spun by hand, with nothing but an oversized wooden top.

The first time I tried spinning, I was amazed at how hard it was. I let go of the spindle to pull some yarn, and it promptly fell to the floor, too heavy for the wisps of wool holding it up. I tried a thicker tuft of fiber, spun the spindle faster, and somehow ended up with a sweaty, matted wad instead of yarn. I'm a little embarrassed to admit that it took me years to learn the method. If my household were depending on me to make cloth to keep them warm in an impending winter, we would have frozen to death.

But one night, it suddenly clicked. I flicked the spindle, pulled the fiber, and watched, mesmerized, as yarn mysteriously grew out of my bundle of wool. My hands had somehow learned what to do. I spun until the spindle was full, spun another batch after that, and plied them together to make my first skein of yarn.

Spindles are elegant tools, but when the spinning wheel was invented—in India, China, or the Middle East, depending on which scholar you ask—everything changed. There are lots of variations, but the spinning wheel's basic design is ingenious. The big wheel that gives the device its name is called the drive wheel. You turn the drive wheel, either with a treadle or by hand, and as it turns, it spins a smaller part that twists the fiber and winds up the finished yarn at the same time. With hand spindles, spinning and winding are two separate steps, so the wheel cuts your spinning time in half. Plus, with spindles, gravity is supposed to be your ally, but sometimes it can be a giant pain in the ass. With spinning wheels, a split second of clumsiness won't send your work rolling across the floor. It's no surprise that by the 13th century, the wheel had swept across Europe.

Now I was reenacting history with my Craigslist search. I emailed the wheel's owner and held my breath, convinced that a mob of spinners was already fighting over it at her door. I whooped when she replied that no one had bought it yet. I drove to Orange County and met my wheel in a suburban home much like the one I'd grown up in. The wheel was beautiful, sleek, and perfect, made of luminous beechwood with decorated spokes. The owner told me it had once been used in a stage production of *Sleeping Beauty*. Now it was mine, mine, mine.

I just had no idea how to use it.

When witches think of spinning, we often think of the *Moirai*, or Fates: the three Greek goddesses who spin, measure, and cut the thread of each person's life. The *Moirai* are archetypal cousins to the Norse Norns, who shape the fate of warriors at the base of Yggdrasil and are also associated with fiber and thread. As Barber points out, the mystery of a new human being coming into existence bears a startling resemblance to thread emerging from the mass of fiber on a distaff. The raw materials of life are given form and meaning; order emerges from chaos. When a spinner spins yarn—then measures and cuts it for a project—they mimic the Fates not just by creating something new, but by closing off all possibilities for it except the one they've decided on.

I suspect that humans have been using spinning for magic since we first learned to do it. Ukrainian-American witch Madame Pamita, in Baba Yaga's Book of Witchcraft, writes about the craft's meditative quality: "If we turn our thoughts and intentions toward the beautiful life we wish to spin for ourselves and our loved ones, we can imbue the yarn or thread with that powerful transformative energy." Spellbooks and grimoires are filled with knot spells and witch's ladders, which lock a witch's intention into the knots in a cord. Thread is used for binding, tying, connecting, severing, and so much more. As Madame Pamita notes, the spiral of thread mimics our DNA. No wonder it's such a powerful symbol.

And it's not just the thread itself that holds magical power. The tools of spinning are also sacred and magical objects. Once, I found a spell that involved using the drive band of a spinning wheel as a binding tool. The drive wheel itself resembles the Wheel of Fortune in the tarot. Norse seeresses were buried with distaffs, and in her novel *The*

*Weaver and the Witch Queen*, Viking Age scholar Genevieve Gornichec imagines them miming the act of spinning as they practice the prophetic magic called seiðr.

But even for the most disciplined witch, spinning carries some chaos with it. Of all the fiber arts I've tried, it's the least predictable. You never know when a wad of tangled fiber may get sucked into your yarn. The yarn itself can vary in width and consistency, even when it's spun by the steadiest hand. Look at thread under a microscope, and you'll see plenty of wayward fibers. Even if the stitches in your knitting are perfect, uniform down to the last millimeter, you'll never spin completely perfect yarn. When I learned to spin, I quickly found that I had to be in a positive mind-set for my yarn to come out right. If I spun while I was stressed or angry, I'd end up with yarn that wasn't fit for a bird's nest.

When I sat down to figure out my new spinning wheel, that positive mind-set was my only asset. Well, that, and a lot of YouTube videos. I watched one video of a woman who, for reasons I'm still not clear on, brought her spinning wheel out to a dock on a riverbank. I watched as she demonstrated how to fasten a length of starter yarn onto the wheel's bobbin and then attach it to her fiber. I rewound the video over and over as she worked the treadle and the fiber turned to yarn. I failed. I cried. I tried again. I cried. I failed. I rewound the video. I tried again.

Eventually, I got the hang of it, but I realized that wheel spinning was more complicated than I'd thought. The drive band had to be tightened or loosened depending on how thick the yarn was going to be. There were different drafting methods: woolen drafting for warmer yarn; worsted for denser, stronger stuff. There were techniques with names like "the long draw" and "spinning in the grease." There was a lot I didn't know. Slowly, with the help of the internet, I learned.

Now that I owned a contraption I was in love with, I found that maintenance was weirdly fun. I noticed a squeaking sound in the wheel's axle, which went away after I oiled it. The drive band wore out, and I learned how to replace it. The procedure was literally just looping a long string and tying it, but when I finished and it worked, I strutted around like I'd landed Apollo 13. I finally understood why some people loved fixing old cars. Soon, I settled into a nightly ritual when I got home from work, spinning in the fifteen minutes or so before we sat down to dinner. The flash of the whirling drive wheel, the gentle hiss of the moving parts, the yarn steadily streaming from my fingers; each night I felt lifelines forming from the tangles of fate.

At first I used a big bag of practice wool my friend had given me, but eventually I bought some nice dyed wool on Etsy. I watched the colors spool onto the bobbin, green fading to brown before brightening to purple and back again, the soft tones of a flowered meadow at twilight. I plied them into four small skeins. When they were finished, I ran them over my cheek, smelled them, squished them in my hands.

I'd been knitting for twenty years, but this yarn felt different. Suddenly I itched to learn something new.

I decided I needed a loom.


## Part 2: The Flip

If spinning is the first stage of creation, bringing form from chaos, then weaving brings that form to its full potential. "One's life-span was conceived by the Greeks as a thread, formed by the Fates at birth,"

Barber writes, "but the act of weaving the thread symbolized what one did with that life, the choices of the individual." Like the warp and weft threads in a loom, we transform each other as our lives intersect. Weaving isn't just central to human civilization; in Western culture, it's become a way of describing human existence.

And we know it, even though the art of weaving has been largely forgotten, and any art form associated with women is inevitably dismissed as a quaint and mindless hobby. Weaving has, well, woven itself into more metaphors than I can count. Once, when I was a teenager, I mused that life felt like a vast tapestry, and felt pretty smart until I found the same sentiment in a hundred different novels and poems. There's a Reclaiming chant that I've sung at more than one public ritual: *Weave and spin, weave and spin / This is how the work begins / Mend and heal, mend and heal / Take the dream and make it real.* In our daily lives, we take weaving (and other textile arts) for granted, throwing on the first shirt we pull out of a drawer in the morning. Deep down, we recognize what a profound act it really is.

Like spinning, weaving is directly tied to witchcraft. (Tied! There's another fiber metaphor.) In Monica Furlong's novel *Wise Child*, an apprentice witch sneaks up to her teacher's attic and discovers a wondrous sight: "a huge upright loom, the threads weighted with stones.... The colors may have clashed and made a painful confusion of effects, but each graded so gently and subtly into the next, or else lay beside a color with which it was in perfect harmony, that the total effect was delightful. It made you feel glad as you looked at it."

You may think weaving is easy until you actually try it. The warp threads sit on the loom, and the weft threads go over and under them, right? In reality, even the simplest-looking weave can be pretty complicated. Dressing a loom can take days. The warp threads have to be stretched tight and threaded through a device called a heddle. Lift up the heddle, and some of the warp threads will be raised to form a space called a shed. To weave a row, the weaver tosses a shuttle containing the weft threads through the shed, and catches it on the other side. They then lower the heddle and beat the new row into place. At the juncture of warp and cloth, potential becomes reality. Threads settle into their new configurations. Patterns and images slowly emerge, row by row, like a story being written. I wanted to learn that kind of magic.

What I wanted was a harness loom: one of the huge looms that can weave fancy patterns. Harness looms are thousands of dollars and the size of dining tables, so that was out of the question. Instead, I settled for a smaller and cheaper kind of loom called a rigid heddle. There was a model called the Schacht Flip, which you could fold up for easy storage. I'd soon learn that using a rigid heddle often involves hacks and workarounds, coaxing the loom to do things it wasn't built for. Someday, I promised myself, I would get the real thing.

This story would be more exciting if I told you that I immediately dressed my loom with the purple and green yarn I'd spun, but I'm happy to report that I have a little common sense. The first thing I made on my new loom was a simple set of dish towels. Those towels taught me all the quirks and oddities of weaving: how to calculate length, how to keep the warps taut and the selvages even, how to fix mistakes and weave in loose ends. It went fine. The towels were beautiful, white with red twill borders that I'd put in by hand, thread by thread. A few months later they were covered in stains, ruined from wiping up some substance I didn't want to guess at. Dish towels are for drying dishes. The only liquid they should ever touch is water. What had happened to them?

It wasn't my family's fault, I grimly told myself. They had no idea how much work I'd put into them. No one ever knows how much work goes into a simple length of cloth.

Next, I turned to the green and purple yarn.

I knew a scarf was my only option, since I'd only spun a few hundred yards of yarn, and even then, it'd be tight. Still, I double-checked my calculations, and it seemed that I would have enough. Knitting uses one continuous length of yarn, so if you come up short, you can always undo the whole thing and make something else. What's scary about most looms, though, is that after you measure your warp threads, you have to cut them with scissors in order to thread them. There's no way around this step. Once your warp length is locked in, the yarn can't be used for anything else. Standing there with my fabric shears, I felt like the Moirai made flesh: If I miscalculated and screwed this up, there was no going back.

Snip. I dressed the loom and began.

In some types of weaving, the weaver's magical intentions are obvious: Talismans and lucky symbols are woven into garments, bringing the wearer protection and prosperity. Look at the skirts and blouses of a peasant outfit, and you'll find roses, birds, eggs, diamonds, lozenges, crosses, and more. In other types of weaving, the magic is as hidden as it is in spinning, with intentions whispered into the newly forming cloth. I didn't know how to weave images yet, so the colors of the yarn did the work of making it beautiful. The warps were bold stripes of purple and green. When I put in the weft, washes of color began

*Witch Blood Rising*

to emerge, like watercolors. In one section, I'd switched from a skein ending with green to a skein beginning with purple, and the transition remained as a sharp knife of color. I held my breath as the scarf was born, row by row. It was going to be as beautiful as I'd hoped.

Then I started running out of yarn.

It was hard to say for sure. But gradually, the first skein of my weft yarn disappeared, and my second began to diminish. Inch by inch I worked, but the yarn seemed to dwindle faster than the inches I had left to go. Please, I thought, please don't let me run out of yarn.

Once, I had a dream in which I was fighting a faceless enemy with a sword, and an owl swooped down to give me a meaningful look. Athena, I thought when I woke up, but I never did anything about it. Athena is famously the goddess of war, but, as Barber points out, she's also the goddess of weaving and countless other crafts and technologies. Put all her jobs together, and she's the goddess of human ingenuity. As I worried that my scarf would be a bust, too short to wear and forever unfinished, I thought of her.

"Athena," I found myself murmuring. "Please, if you give me enough yarn to finish this scarf, I'll think of you whenever I wear it!"

It's not the kind of deal you want to make with a goddess, especially a goddess with whom you've never established any kind of relationship, especially when that goddess has a reputation for turning people who offend her into spiders. How do you know you'll never put it on while distracted, forgetting to toss her a thought? But the words came out of my mouth before I fully understood what I was saying.

I ended up with enough yarn to finish the scarf. In fact, despite how tiny the skein looked at the end, I had enough left over to knit a matching hat. Fiber artists tend to give our projects names, so I named my scarf Athena. I'm wearing my Athena scarf as I type these words, as an offering to the goddess of wisdom, and a reminder of what my two hands were able to create.

There's another dream I once had, around the same time Athena visited me.

In the dream, I found a small wooden box, painted in bright colors. The words *witch tools* were written on the lid. I didn't know where the box came from, but I knew it was for me. I opened it. It was filled with dozens of steel tapestry needles.

A short time after the dream, I found a tapestry needle on the sidewalk. I kept it safe for years, and then used it to bind off the edges of my Athena scarf.

But the needles in that box weren't just for stitching hems. I've lost count of the ways I use fiber arts tools in my witchcraft: embroidering charm bags, spinning thread for knot spells, sewing altar cloths, weaving ritual shawls. Fiber arts and witchcraft are plied together like the strands in a length of yarn, like the DNA of hidden histories. The needle, the spindle, the distaff, the wheel, the shuttle, the loom: They're all witches' tools. They're all tools of creation.

I'll confess that I get irrationally annoyed at how many spinning and weaving metaphors there are in modern witchcraft, considering how few witches actually know how to do it. It reminds me of Marian Green's admonition, in *A Witch Alone*, against dull athames: "There is no place in modern magic for blunt blades, either symbolically or practically." If you want to invoke something magically, you should know how to do it physically. Otherwise, how can you really understand the power you're tapping into? It's like trying to describe a place you've never visited.

So try it, if you're able to. Pick up an embroidery needle, or a set of knitting needles, or a crochet hook. Make a lap loom out of cardboard. Buy a beginner's spindle and a bag of fiber, if you're feeling ambitious. Let the yarn slip against your fingers. Loop it around a needle, beat a row into place, and watch a story form.

## A Spell to Weave a Story

For this spell, you'll need a square of stiff cardboard eight inches wide and ten inches tall. This isn't a metaphor. I'm not talking about astral cardboard. I'm inviting you to actually do this.

Cut a row of slits along the top and bottom edges of the cardboard, ¼ of an inch apart. They'll look like fringe, but they don't need to be deep—just big enough to hold some yarn in place. Oh, right—you'll need some yarn. As many colors and textures as you want. Honestly? The more, the better. What you make may look terrible, or it may be the most beautiful thing in the world. How will you know until you try?

Take one length of yarn and wrap it around your little loom, wedging it into each slit. Wrap it until every slit is filled, if you like, or stop part of the way through and switch to a different color. When you're finished, the front and back of your loom will look like the fretboard of a guitar. These are your warps.

You know how weaving is done: over and under, over and under. Take a length of yarn—your weft—and weave it into the warps near the bottom of one side of the loom. Leave a bit hanging off the end; you can tuck it into the back when you're done. When the yarn comes out the other side, turn it around and weave it back in the other way. Under and over, under and over.

Switch colors whenever you want. Play with different sequences: two over and one under, for instance. Experiment and solve problems. Make mistakes. Undo them if you want, or leave them. Nothing in the world is perfect.

Whisper your story into the tapestry as you weave it. Whisper the story of who you were and who you are. Whisper your intention for who you'll become. Find yourself in your weaving, a thread among other threads, touching and changing its world as it goes along, over and under, back and forth. Notice the changing colors, the emerging shapes, the thing you're creating.

When your weft reaches the top of the loom—or when you decide that you're finished—cut the warps in the middle of the other side of the loom. Tie them off like the tassels of a rug, and trim them down. You can tie one end to a wooden dowel and hang your weaving on the wall, or you can use it as a tiny altar cloth. You made it. You told this story. It's yours.

Or maybe, now that you've birthed it, it belongs to itself: a tiny world with even more stories to tell.

# 8

## Granny Datura

### Learning herbalism on the screen
### and in the dirt

At first, COVID felt like a kind of very scary vacation. That very first weekend, when all the shops and restaurants shut down, the people of Los Angeles flocked to the parks instead. The playgrounds all over the city overflowed with children, and every grill smoked with burgers and hot dogs. The city, appalled at our bone-deep stupidity, promptly shut down the parks, too. Our two-bedroom condo began to feel like a pressure cooker. The school district offered a summer camp over Zoom. We declined.

But one day in July, our neighbors texted us. They'd found an open campground an hour north of the city! Did we want to go with them? I almost cried, I was so happy. How was it possible? I didn't care. I craved a night under the moon, bathed in owl cries and coyote howls. I packed supplies to build an altar, some sacred bits and bobs that wouldn't break if they were jostled in the car. The haze of quarantine and homeschooling had domesticated me. I wanted to feel feral again.

The highway leading to the campground was surrounded by harsh, rocky land, covered in the sun-bleached dry grasses of summer. We passed swaths of land that were burned from wildfires, dotted with skeletal trees. Which fire had this been? Had it even gotten a name? I couldn't keep up with them all.

Eventually, we spotted a sign for the campground. We pulled into a parking lot and I felt a jolt of dismay. This wasn't an actual campground at all—it was just a patchy lawn with some tents and dirt bikes around the edges. In the middle was a huge plaster tipi, and some kids playing with squirt guns. I'd been picturing woods, trails, streams. Oaks and pines and poppies. This was crabgrass and asphalt. My older daughter had sunk into a kind of fugue state during the drive, but she roused herself to peer out the car window. "Is this it?" she cried. "I don't want to camp here! I thought we were going to the place with the waterfall!"

The place with the waterfall was, of course, closed. "Let's not whine," said my husband, as stricken as the rest of us.

"But it's so *ugly!*" she wailed. My younger one, picking up on her sister's mood, began to kick and fuss in her car seat. It was eleven a.m., and the temperature was in the nineties.

My husband went into the office to sign in while one of the campers climbed on a dirt bike and began to rev it up. A minute later, my husband ran out, triumphant. "This isn't it!" he crowed. "This is the wrong campground! We're at the wrong one!"

"Girls!" I yelled. "Did you hear that? We're leaving!"

"*Yay!*" they shouted in unison.

We took off like we'd robbed the place. I stared out the window at the shimmering heat. We passed a huge RV park and the sea of white roofs blinded me until I looked away. I would get my woods and my streams! I would dance under the stars!

"That's weird," my husband said, frowning at Google Maps. "It's saying to turn around."

We made a U-turn a mile later and came back. Ahead of me I could see the trailer park. *Turn in 500 feet,* Google said, and a dark knowledge began to form in me.

I could see the driveway, the RVs wavering behind it. *Your destination is on the left.* "No," I said.

We passed it again. *Make a U-turn,* Google said.

Five minutes later we pulled into the parking lot. The so-called campground was just a front office with a thousand RVs in a grid. We texted our neighbors in the faint hope that there had been a massive misunderstanding, that maybe there was a third campground tucked away somewhere, but no. "Don't worry, they have tent camping!" our neighbors cheerfully texted back. "It's in the very back! Just drive past all the trailers! We're running late!"

So we drove past the trailers, and found ourselves in a dusty ravine bordered by tall piles of industrial junk. There were rusted pipes and diggers that looked like set dressing for a *Terminator* movie. A few people were indeed setting up tents. We leapt for a shady spot and felt proud of ourselves, sitting at a picnic table under one of the only trees around, but when we started unloading the car, the group in the spot across from us set up a giant speaker system and began blasting music. One camper plugged in a microphone so he could emcee. We moved to the other end of the ravine, to a spot in full sun. It was almost a hundred degrees out, and we were expected to spend forty-eight hours here. My husband and I briefly talked about leaving, but our neighbors hadn't arrived yet and we were too damn polite to go through with it.

We unloaded the car and set up the tent. The ground was so hard that the tent pegs wouldn't go in, so we resorted to piling rocks on top of the loops in the hopes that they'd hold. I sorted through my things and found a first aid salve that I'd made from the calendula and plantain I grew in pots outside my door, steeping them in oil and then mixing them with beeswax. I'd brought it in case of a scraped knee or a scratch from a thorn, but I couldn't think of where to put it where it wouldn't melt in the heat. I finally tucked it into a corner of the trunk of the car.

Standing back up, I saw my toddler wandering into a mass of dry bramble. I hurried to get her out, thinking about snakes and ticks, and I noticed a fetid, pondlike smell drifting from whatever lay beyond the branches. As I lifted her out and set her back on the dirt, I saw something: Huge, velvety green leaves dotted with trumpet-like white blossoms. Some flowers were still tightly curled; others were already wilted. Prickly green seed pods swelled underneath rotting petals. *Datura*,[9] I thought, and knelt down to greet her.

---

9. Like the botanist Robin Wall Kimmerer, I capitalize *Datura* when I'm referring to the overarching spirit of that plant and use lowercase (datura) when referring to individual plants.

Like the witch, Datura is often seen as a thorny weed, a noxious intruder with no claim to the space she occupies, and that hatred is a clue to the power she holds. In Europe, she's known as Devil's Trumpet, Devil's Apple, Devil's Herb, Devil's Snare, and Devil's Cucumber—names that point to her reputation as one of the premier witching herbs. Native to North America but naturalized in Europe in the 1500s, Datura "gives to witches the power of riding in the air on a broomstick," according to Richard Folkard's 1892 *Plant Lore, Legends, and Lyrics*. Those who ingest enough of her fall into a stupor, seemingly leaving their bodies as they experience visions. The alkaloids in Datura are considered hallucinogens, but that's not quite accurate. They're actually deliriants. I've heard of people taking Datura recreationally, but a datura trip is not a safe or fun activity. A dose big enough to fly you to the Sabbat can also suppress your respiratory system and put you into a coma, if it doesn't kill you.

But the witching herbs are known for their ability to both harm and heal, and Datura is no different. Herbalist Maud Grieve, for instance, wrote in the 1930s about Datura's ability to relieve spasmodic coughs and inflammatory pain, touting her as "a better cough-remedy than opium." Arguably the best authorities on Datura are the Indigenous herbalists who work with her, like the Chumash People of Southern California, who know her as Momoy. According to Chumash lore, Momoy was a matron before the great flood turned her into a white-blossomed plant. There's a traditional Datura infusion, toloache, which is used by both medicine workers and laypeople to achieve spirit flight, break curses, and treat physical ailments. But the same Puritanical mind-set that made my ancestors associate her with the Devil is still at work in North America. In 2017,

Indigenous-owned Desert Monsoon Apothecary tried to sell datura pain salve on Etsy but found the listing promptly banned by Etsy's "integrity team," which accused them of peddling recreational drugs.

Over the years, as I began to dabble in herbalism, I started noticing Datura everywhere. I spotted her in neglected spaces: the edge of a vacant lot, the median of a busy street, the dirt by the dumpsters at Griffith Park. I saw her on hiking trails, too, but usually she was a weed, springing up when landowners weren't looking, and they quickly ripped her out because of her toxicity. The irony is that common ornamentals like daffodils and foxgloves are just as deadly, yet people go to great pains to cultivate them. What a powerful metaphor: a matriarch rich with medicinal and spiritual gifts, demonized and cast to the margins.

One of my quarantine activities, which I took on to give some meaning to days filled with homeschooling and doomscrolling, was an online certificate course in herbalism. If I completed the course's ten modules, the website promised, I'd be a bona fide folk herbalist, equipped to treat any little ailments that may crop up in my family. I fantasized about following in Bubby Esther's footsteps. I would become a modern-day folks froi, a true wise woman, a hedge witch in every sense. Neighbors would probably come to me for remedies and advice. I'd have to keep odd hours. It would be a burden and a gift.

But I was two modules into the course, and it was already a disappointment. It was all generic wellness industry junk, multivitamin recommendations and paleo recipes and screeds against cooking with salt. All the information on herbs was riddled with pseudoscience and New Age platitudes. What did I expect? It was a cheap online course.

A "certified folk herbalist" was an oxymoron. I was never going to learn to work with plants by completing online modules.

Despite the embarrassing stuff in the course, I knew from experience how effective herbs could be. I soothed insect bites with plantain and sore throats with sage. I took chamomile for anxiety and hops for insomnia. My knowledge of herbs felt piecemeal, though. Not good enough, not confident enough, not encyclopedic enough. I was afraid that if I ever practiced herbalism on someone else, I'd mess up and kill them. I couldn't shake the feeling that herbs worked like pills, and you had to check a giant database for interactions.

At the campsite, I looked up from the datura plant I was communing with and saw three more scattered around a little clearing. There were tall stands of mugwort, too, another renowned witching herb. Further back, there was an intriguing gap in the trees, and I suspected, despite the algae smell, that it hid something I wanted to see. I stood, and took a step.

My older kid ran up to me. "There's a clubhouse!" she said. "And a wading pool! Can we go? Can we go, please?"

I had a friend, another witch, who liked to go camping every single weekend. That was how she was able to form relationships with the plant world and perform rituals in the woods. But she didn't have kids, and I had two.

I picked my way out of the bramble and went to my children.

We went to find the clubhouse. At the edge of the campground, the ravine narrowed into a sandy wash that pulled at our shoes, and I soon realized that we were tramping through the remains of the Santa Clara River. I couldn't believe it: The place was actually pretty.

Whole plant communities had sprouted since the river dried up. I found more mugwort, vast patches of silvery stalks brimming with flower buds, and full-grown walnut trees, and, of course, more datura. I could see the roofs of the RVs over the riverbank, but this little strip of land was a forgotten place, made inconvenient by the sand and the embankment, free from litter and footprints. I was intrigued by the mugwort and datura growing side by side, since mugwort is a water lover and datura thrives in heat. Maybe their root systems reached to different depths, with the datura hanging out at the surface while the mugwort stretched deeper for a part of the river that still flowed underground. Or maybe the riverbed was a sweet spot between two ecosystems, a borderland where both plants could thrive.

We climbed out of the riverbed onto a broad lawn, and I found the strangest sight yet. The clubhouse was overrun by a huge mob of ravens, clicking and chuckling in the eucalyptus trees and flying in slow cyclones above us. There were hundreds of birds, maybe a thousand, and the grass was littered with shed feathers and gobs of poop. We crept underneath their ungodly racket and sat on a basketball court with a few other families, where a staff member was starting a round of Bingo. None of us won. When the temperature topped 110, the girls rolled listlessly in the wading pool for a few minutes before declaring the water too cold.

That evening, our neighbors finally rolled in as we were sitting down for an outdoor screening of *Pirates of the Caribbean*. Their daughter joined us on our blanket as they went to pitch their tent in the twilight. "Look," I said, pointing at the silhouettes wheeling and tumbling above us. "Bats!"

My older kid tore her eyes away from the movie and squinted at the sky. After a minute, she scoffed. "Those aren't bats!" she said. "Those are just birds." She simply couldn't believe that something as mythical as a real live bat might be here, right above us. There are bats in Los Angeles, of course, but they're hard to spot, and children are rarely outside at night to look for them.

I sighed and sat back on the blanket. I was too tired to argue. Back in the ravine, the datura blossoms would be opening right about now, presenting themselves to hawkmoths for pollination. I was sad to miss it.

Normally I can make it until morning before needing to pee, but when the only bathroom is a vault toilet fifty feet away in pitch darkness, I inevitably need to get up in the middle of the night. That night, I trudged to the bathroom and stopped on my way back to take in the stars. I couldn't quite see the Milky Way, not this close to the city, but I did pick out Scorpius behind the trees. When I got back to the tent, I found that no one was sleeping.

As I lay there, the night gradually came alive with hoots and screeches. "What are those?" my older kid said.

There was a low *hoo-hoo-WOO, hoo-hoo*. "That's a great horned owl," I said.

The call was answered by several screeches. "And those are the baby owls!" I added.

Somewhere in the campsite, a car honked its horn. "And that's a car owl," I said. Everyone laughed, and I grinned at my own joke in the dark.

The next day, I woke up in a furnace. My husband was out of the tent already, and the girls were scrabbling around on top of their sleeping bags in some inscrutable game. I peeled off my own bag, damp with sweat, and checked the temperature on my phone. It was already almost a hundred out.

There was no shelter anywhere. The tent was a nonstarter, and the clubhouse was shuttered because of COVID. Even the front office didn't allow anyone in without official business. We hurriedly ate breakfast and took the girls to the wading pool, but as the temperature soared higher and higher, there was only so much wading anyone could stand. By lunchtime we found ourselves sitting in a miserable little row along the shade cast by a spindly tree, at a loss for what to do.

Our neighbors folded down the back seats of their hatchback, crawled in, and turned on their engine to run the air conditioner. Soon my older kid crawled in after them. My toddler began to cry, her face flushed, and my husband and I fretted about heatstroke. We did the only rational thing we could think of: We strapped her into our own car, asked the neighbors to watch our other kid, and drove away.

I feel guilty enough burning fossil fuels when I need to get to work. But going for a drive on a camping trip? Sacrilege. We spent the whole ride assuring ourselves that we weren't bad people. A few months after the trip, I would read Kim Stanley Robinson's climate change novel *The Ministry for the Future*, which opens on a nightmarish heat wave in India. People are already dying at the beginning of the book, but then, as the heat keeps spiraling, the electrical grid buckles under the pressure and the power goes out. That means no air-conditioning, and the entire town ends up dead. For now, the novel is mostly science fiction, but heat waves already kill people around the world. While we weathered our unpleasant camping trip, the city was operating cooling centers where people could sit in the A/C and receive free bottles of water. Everyone knew Los Angeles was becoming less and less habitable, but no one ever wanted to talk about it.

The car ride and the cool air lulled the toddler into a nap on the highway. I asked Google to find us coffee, and soon we parked in a strip mall, where we sat in the car and sipped Starbucks drinks and complained. Across the street there was a housing development flanked by the same tropical shrubs that adorned my street growing up: oleanders, ficuses, and birds of paradise, kept alive in the desert with unimaginable amounts of imported water. Compared to the ferocious landscape we'd just left, the lush green lawns and palm trees outside the houses reminded me of a terraformed colony you may see in a sci-fi movie, a perfect circle of green with a big glass dome on top.

We did everything we could to avoid going back to the RV park. There was a supermarket in the strip mall, and when the toddler woke up, we racked our brains until we could think of some groceries to buy that wouldn't rot in the heat. Chips, maybe. Crackers.

We drifted through the aisle of the store, listlessly tossing dry goods into the cart, and by the time we got back to the campsite, the temperature had sunk to the nineties. It was a relief after the hundreds, like a cloudburst on a muggy day, and that scared me.

After dinner, as the girls played in the dirt, I went back to the datura. Last night's blossoms had withered, but now I was here at twilight, and the new ones were just beginning to open. If the owners of the RV park ever noticed Datura growing here, they would almost certainly throw her in the dumpster. After all, who wants to risk the liability? Especially with kids around? But for now, she was here, and plentiful and thriving.

Go to a sunny meadow—or a vacant lot, or an overgrown roadside—without any botanical knowledge, and you'll probably see a uniform carpet of green. You might pick out different shades, notice some flowers or odd leaf shapes, but, most likely, nothing will stand out to you.

Learn about just one edible or medicinal plant, though, and suddenly you'll start seeing it everywhere. Learn about three, and the green world will open up to you a little more. Devote yourself to the study of plants, and nature will explode in countless different personalities.

California ecosystems are sometimes harsher than more verdant places. Whenever I go back east, I'm bowled over by the cornucopia around me, all the lush green plants, all the mushrooms. Once, in an alley behind an airport hotel in Boston, I found mugwort, wild carrot, plantain, dandelion, red clover, and St. John's wort all within ten feet of each other. By contrast, the arid hills and basins of Southern California can be prickly, temperamental, even forbidding. You have to earn your medicine here.

Still, I feel bad for all the people who can't casually smell a stand of white sage on a hiking trail, or look at oceans of California poppies in the spring, or drop a sprig of redwood into hot water for tea. This land is often drier and browner than others, but there's so much treasure here. True herbalism—medicinal or magical—isn't just matching a bottle of tincture to an ailment, or rubbing scented oil on a candle.

It's learning to live and work alongside these treasures, these partners, these friends.

Los Angeles County is so crowded that if even a tiny portion of its population took to foraging for wild plants, they would pick it clean. That means I do basically no foraging, as much as I'd like to. My one exception, though, is weeds. Isn't it interesting that some of the plants most useful to humans always pop up in disturbed areas, right around human settlements? And isn't it tragic that we're in such a rush to stamp them out?

I had a pair of embroidery scissors with me, and I got them out of the car. I combed my fingers through my hair, and when a few loose hairs came out, I set them at the base of the datura plant as an offering: part of me for part of her. Then I clipped three small sprigs of new growth from spots I knew would recover quickly. When we got home the next day, I would infuse them into salve, along with mugwort, elderflower, yarrow, and clary sage. It wouldn't be a true flying ointment. I didn't have the training to make one safely, I hadn't harvested enough to render it psychoactive, and most of the alkaloids are in the seeds anyway. But I could use the salve ritualistically before meditation or dream incubation, rubbing it into my wrists and throat, inviting Datura to join me in my rites. "Thank you," I said.

I stood up to find my neighbor jogging toward me. "We've got a bee sting," she said.

*I turn my back for five minutes,* I thought. I hurried over and learned that my older kid had sat on a bee. My neighbor and I inspected the welt on her leg, and I remembered the calendula and plantain salve in the trunk. It was mostly liquid from the heat, but my daughter calmed down when I spread some on the sting. Soon she was back to playing. Later I would learn that baking soda is actually a better remedy for bee stings—it neutralizes the acid in the venom—but an herbalist is always learning.

I put the salve back and spread the datura sprigs on the dashboard to start drying. "Mind if I wander?" I asked my husband.

He said he'd watch the kids. Our neighbors had gotten out a karaoke microphone, and the kids were taking turns belting out Taylor Swift songs.

I went back to the bramble, and as the sun went down and the air cooled, I finally picked my way through to see what was on the other side. The fetid smell grew stronger, and I came to a hidden creek speckled with scarlet monkeyflowers and evening primroses. I walked along its edge, and the trees on the other side fell away to reveal a hillside covered in grand mason sage. Here was a tiny patch of what this land had looked like before its mutilation, a palette of greens and grays with euphoric pops of wildflowers. Much of the creek was stagnant, which explained the smell, but I took it all in as I walked.

After a few minutes, I came out into a quiet meadow, surrounded by oaks and more sage, and filled—here I actually gasped—with mounds and mounds of datura. There was a derelict building off in the distance and the faint sounds of traffic from the highway, but this tiny meadow was peaceful and untouched. I wandered among the plants reverently, stroking leaves, studying seed pods. It was twilight now, and somewhere in the branches above me the owls we'd heard the night before started calling to each other again. My altar tools still lay in my bag in the car, where they would stay until I unpacked them at home the next day. You don't always get to set up your altar, but sometimes you get something even better.

For years now, I've seen Datura as a grandmother. Partly it's because of the Chumash myth. Once I saw her as a matron, I couldn't unsee it even if I wanted to. The land speaks a language of symbols to us, tells us its stories in archetypes and myths, and, if you listen, you'll find that some stories resonate across time and culture.

Mostly, though, it's because Datura, like the witch she aids, flourishes at the margins—by the dumpsters, by the industrial junk, on the crumbling edges of lawn and pavement. She's the wilderness that refuses to go away. She lives her life in the little-noticed spaces, cultivating the powers of the healer and mystic. Weeds are so much more interesting than ornamentals.

Standing in that meadow, I decided to drop out of the herbalism course. I'd find another way to learn.

I got up from one of the datura plants and stretched my back. I'd been gone too long and it was time to go back to the kids. But then I saw movement in a tree up ahead. I froze and squinted, and the thing moved again, a flash of golden haunches and paddlelike paws, and I saw that it was a bobcat jumping through the branches of an oak. I'd never seen a bobcat in the wild before, never in all my years of living here.

In the stillness, I heard the karaoke microphone echoing through the trees. I stood in awe of that damaged holy place, drinking it in while I could, knowing that if I ever came back, it might be gone.

## A Spell to Find a Teacher Among the Weeds

Stand at the threshold of your home looking out, and open the door. You'll want to take note of *which* home you're starting in. Location is everything in this spell.

Take a step over the threshold, pick a direction, and walk for a while. Now that the spell is underway, you'll eventually notice a path you've never seen before. It may be grand and gilded, so obvious that you're amazed you never spotted it. It may be tiny and tucked away, hidden around a corner or obscured by an over-grown shrub. That's what happens when you get to know a place too well: You stop seeing its secret places, and you stop hearing its voices.

Well, obviously you'll need to follow this new path. Isn't it funny, how many secrets a familiar place can hold? How the longer you spend somewhere, the thicker a veil it seems to wear? Make sure you walk slowly and take in everything. There are countless creatures living here, and some of them may venture out to meet you. Learn their names. Return their greetings. Give them some space if it looks like they need it, but whatever you do, don't ignore them.

Stroll until you find the place where civilization peters out, where the asphalt is cracked and the sidewalk is buckled, or where the dirt trail turns into a deer path and fades away altogether. This is the hinterland where your teacher lives. This is where you'll find the hedge that holds magic and wisdom.

Your teacher will be growing at the very end of your journey. When you recognize them, kneel to meet them. Take note of the shape of their leaves, the arc of their stems. Ask them if they have flowers or fruit. Draw a portrait of them. Compose a poem or sing them into a song. If they give you permission, take a bit of them home with you. Your teacher has a thousand things to teach you, so let them make their introduction.

Take a long look around you before you head back. This shabby, crumbling place where weeds thrive and insects hum? This is where witchery lives. This is where the deepest lessons are taught. You just need senses sharp enough and a mind keen enough to catch them, and a heart that's brave enough to let them in.

# 9

# The Bee Priestess

## On urban wildlife and responsibilities of the witch

Datura is one priestess of the land. There are countless others all around us.

There's a neighborhood I like to walk in, close to the blocky apartment buildings and loud music on my street, but filled with trees and wildlife. It's one of the richest neighborhoods in Los Angeles, and when I walk, I like to study the mansions and guess how many families could fit in each one. How many households could we squeeze into this or that mansion, if the whole neighborhood was converted into communes? Sometimes I grudgingly admire the gardens that hold native plants and imagine how I'd redesign the ones that don't. I'll touch the bark of ash trees and cypresses, and in summer, I'll listen for the *chit-chit-chit-chit-chit* of nesting Cooper's hawks. I don't know how the wealthy residents see their own neighborhood, but, to me, it's an urban forest. The real residents are the birds and animals and insects, with the mansions receding into the landscape like boulders.

It was on one of my walks that I first found the bees. I noticed movement at my feet one day, and paused to watch a couple of bees fly into a hole at the base of a camphor tree. I knelt, delighted at my find, and watched a steady stream of bees landing and launching, hovering as they adjusted speed and trajectory, crawling in and out of the crevices behind the exposed roots and fallen leaves. One of the few things I love more than watching bees forage is finding a honeybee hive and imagining the hidden city inside.

Almost all honeybees are female.[10] Males, or drones, perform precisely one task in their entire lifetime—impregnating a new queen—and that task ends midflight when their penis comes off with an audible pop and hangs from the body of their airborne mate. The hive, for the most part, is a massive community of sisters: sisters scouting out flowers, gathering pollen, building and repairing the comb, and feeding their larval siblings. Even the queen herself is the sister of the workers, if she's young enough. I suspect I spend a ridiculous amount of time thinking about communes.

The hive became one of the stops on my walks, along with the hawk nest, and I soon learned that I wasn't the only person who had noticed the colony. One day, I found a note taped to the wall by the tree: STOP STUFFING GASOLINE-SOAKED RAGS IN THE

---

10. I learned many of my bee facts from *The Bee: A Natural History* by Noah Wilson-Rich. Also, my friend Lila Amanita, a witch and biologist who knows everything there is to know about insects, fact-checked the original version of this chapter. Any mistakes are mine alone.

BEE NEST. I peered into the hive, alarmed, and saw there was none of the usual traffic around the entrance. *Oh, no,* I thought, as if someone had stuffed gasoline-soaked rags into my own front door, but when I knelt to take a closer look, I saw that there were still a few bees coming in and out of the entrance. I didn't know anything about bees, but I hoped the colony could bounce back. These bees were my neighbors, just like the hawks and the humans. How would you feel if someone came and assaulted your neighbors?

The bees' numbers plummeted over the next few days. Another, more frantic note told people to walk on the other side of the street if they were allergic. I was tied up with work and the kids, but when I did finally make it back out to the hive, what I saw broke me. The notes had been ripped off the wall. The entrance to the hive had been plastered over with mud, and there were hundreds of bodies scattered on the sidewalk.

One hive can contain up to eighty thousand workers, and those workers pollinate countless plants. All the gardens and flower beds on the street, all those expensive cultivars raising home values—none of them could bloom without bees. Did these people want oranges on their orange trees? Did they want their roses to bloom? How did they think this all worked? Every day, it seemed, I had to watch people destroy other living beings with a determination I seldom see humans apply to anything else. The COVID death toll in the US was approaching a hundred thousand while people refused to wear masks, there were demonstrations in the streets over the murders of Black people at the hands of cops, and yet another round of wildfires was raging north of the city. Everywhere in my neighborhood, despite all the alarm bells ringing about climate change and the need for more urban forests, people were cutting down trees, tearing out plants, and replacing them with turf and concrete. Then, when their unhoused neighbors tried to set up tents, they protected that turf and concrete with chain-link fences. My rage felt like a dream in which you try to scream and yell, you try to release the frantic anger inside you, but only a hoarse croak emerges.

The ancient Greek and Roman world contained multiple goddesses who fell under what archaeologists call a "mother goddess type"—a goddess associated with fertility and the natural world. Many of these goddesses, including Artemis and Demeter, were closely associated with bees. Their surviving iconography includes numerous images of bees, and the priestesses who served them were called *Melissai*, Greek for "bees." I think I vaguely assumed, at one point, that the Melissai literally worshipped bees, but the name seems to have been metaphorical. Bees were associated with purity, celibacy, and obedience, traits that were expected of priestesses in certain orders. The bee was also closely associated with the fecundity of the natural world, like a field awash in flowers, or a garden bursting with edibles.

Even aside from the associations that we know date from antiquity, the bee is a fitting symbol of the Great Goddess. The entrance to the hive is womblike, hidden away in tree trunks and other hollows. Inside, where no light penetrates, the workers communicate by touch, smell, and vibration as they build their comb and make their honey and tend to their brood. Within the hubbub, the eternally pregnant queen lays egg after egg after egg, a seemingly immortal figure to the generations of workers who maintain the hive around her. After all, a queen can live up to five years, while a worker may die after only a few weeks. As classicist Rachel D. Carlson notes, the bee is like Persephone, flying from the black depths of the hive to the bright blooming meadow and back again. She's both chthonic and celestial, equally at home underground and in the air. Also, like the goddess, she has a dark side: her potentially deadly sting. The bee is a giver of life and a bringer of death.

Then there's the magic of honey. Humans have been collecting honey since at least the Neolithic era, and it predates wine as an offering to the gods. Honey doesn't just have a thousand culinary uses—it's also an antimicrobial healing agent. A dollop can soothe a burn or help clear up a sore throat. The herbalist Rosemary Gladstar has a recipe for medicinal onion-infused honey that her family supposedly kept simmering on the stove all winter long.

Given the wonder of honey, it's no surprise that many religious traditions see it as a metaphor for wisdom and divine love. St. Francis de Sales was struck by the alchemy of the honey-making process, writing, "Watch a bee hovering over the mountain thyme;—the juices it gathers are bitter, but the bee tursns them all to honey,—and so tells the worldling, that though the decent soul finds bitter herbs along its path of devotion, they are all turned to sweetness and pleasantness as it treads." When I studied Yiddish, my teacher told us that in the old days, yeshiva boys learned the aleph-beys by licking the shapes of letters drawn on plates with honey. The ritual emphasized the sweet nourishment of learning, and it was probably a lot more fun than a worksheet.

It seems to have been mainly the bees' production of honey, rather than the bees themselves, that our ancestors saw as sacred. Even with their keen observation, they didn't know how deeply connected bees are to what we recognize as the natural world. Bees evolved alongside the first angiosperms, or flowering plants, and each life-form nudged the other along its evolutionary path. Flowers grew bigger and showier to attract more pollinators, and bees' bodies and behavior continually adapted to the changes in the flowers. Without bees and other bugs, flowers wouldn't exist, at least not in their present form.

I first heard about Colony Collapse Disorder, in which all the worker bees in a hive suddenly disappear, when it was just starting to make the news around 2005. These days, the number of cases has gone down, although researchers still don't know exactly what causes it. Back then, there was serious speculation about the world's food supply collapsing if the bees disappeared, especially because countless crops are pollinated by bee colonies that are rented out to farmers. It's strange to think that our ancestors took pollination for granted and considered honey precious, when now, the exact opposite is true. Go to any supermarket and you'll find rows and rows of honey, in plastic squeezy bears and fancy glass jars, flavored with sage or orange blossom, some of it cut with corn syrup, some of it gourmet. Go to a county fair or old-timey candy store and you can get plastic tubes of it to suck on. Go to a posh farmer's market and you can get some with a hunk of comb inside and a hemp cord tied in a bow around the rim. Even I take honey for granted, grabbing bottles of it off the store shelf to squeeze onto bread for the girls. I do try to remember to say a prayer of thanks to the bees and to the Goddess as I watch it soak into the crumb of toast. I try, but in the scramble of weekday mornings with the school late bells looming, I often forget.

Once, when I lived in another part of town, my neighbor found a single bee on his balcony and came to warn me that our neighborhood, which contained countless flowering trees and shrubs, was also home to bees. "I mean, of course I killed it," he told me. Oh, of course. Of course you did. What else could you possibly do? Be reasonable and ignore it?

I had thought that everyone knew not to kill bees on sight, but I was naive. I had forgotten that, in hanging out with other witches and nature lovers, I lived in a bubble within a culture that's hostile to nature. I'm sure my neighbor had at least one bottle of honey in his kitchen. Maybe his Hebrew teacher had even had him lick a sticky honey aleph from a plate when he was young. I thought of the jacaranda tree next to our building, which glittered with bees every spring when it exploded in purple flowers. What would my neighbor do if he ever noticed it? I took bleak solace in the fact that he would probably never look closely enough at the tree to see it.

Many people I've met over the years have felt very comfortable in a hierarchy, even when they find themselves at the bottom of it. Everyone in that building hated our landlady, but when my husband and I tried to start a tenants' association, no one showed up at the meeting. Why are we so amenable to subjugation? For generations in Europe, honeybees were used as a symbol of monarchy, on the belief that the queen was a leader who commanded her workers. In reality, the queen, drones, and workers all engage in mutual sacrifice for the good of the colony. After her mating flight, the queen can never leave the hive again. Her workers, unable to reproduce, enjoy freedom of movement and the warmth of sunlight. Decisions like where to forage or which site to select for a new hive are democratic, with scouts reporting their finds to the group, which in turn decides collectively what to do.

It would be very easy for me to say, here, that humans should try to be more like bees. But the human mind is organized very differently from that of a bee, and there's not much point in claiming that we can solve our problems by pretending to be another species. Octavia E. Butler elegantly pinpointed the peculiar nature of our minds in her novel *Dawn*: We're both intelligent and hierarchical, and those two traits are fundamentally incompatible. The urge to dominate other beings doesn't mesh with our perception of that urge as unjust. Instead of either an unquestioned hierarchy or an egalitarian society, we get violent power struggles—which, in *Dawn*, lead to a nuclear holocaust. Some human civilizations have figured out how to rein in egos and power grabs. Others haven't.

Humans can't become bees, but we can follow a path that bees have laid out. Bees originally evolved from predatory wasps that, for whatever reason, decided to stop killing, and that's why we now have roses and poppies and lupines and jasmine. A philosophy of nonviolence led to a planet full of flowers. Based on what I know about Indigenous cultures—namely, the immense power of simply acknowledging that other lives, human and nonhuman, are important—a similar outcome doesn't seem impossible for those of us who were raised within the capitalist hierarchies of Western civilization.

Whether we can manage it before the culmination of climate change is another matter. Some scientists believe that we're in the middle of the Earth's sixth mass extinction event, with dozens of species going extinct every single day. But, sure, if you see a bee minding its own business, kill it.

Over time, the mud gradually fell off the hive entrance, but the hole remained vacant. Summer tipped into fall, and the urban forest struggled through heat waves and Santa Ana winds.

*Witch Blood Rising*

There's a curious bit of folklore, which has made its way into some myths, that bees don't reproduce sexually, but rather arise from the carcasses of bulls. In reality, when bees seek to form a new hive, they leave their colony and swarm. We think of swarms of bees as aggressive, predatory superorganisms, but actually they're quite docile—so much so that beekeepers can literally scoop a swarm into an empty hive with their bare hands. With no honeycombs to keep up their strength and no hive to protect, the bees quietly cling to whatever perch they find until their scouts find a site for the new colony.

Did anyone notice the swarm that found the empty hive in the camphor tree? Or did the tree itself seem to birth the bees, little priestesses emerging from their mother's womb? All I know is that one day, when I paused by the tree for what had become a sullen little mourning ritual, I saw bees flying in and out. A small miracle had occurred. The colony had been reborn.

A new note appeared on the wall: *If you do not like the bees, please use the other side of the street. Thank you.* Soon, others followed. On a heart-shaped piece of red paper: *Thank you for protecting the bees!* On bee-themed stationary: *We walk every morning and dearly love seeing the bees. It fills our hearts with happiness and is a wonderful way to begin the day! Thank you!* Someone contributed an entire page of bee jokes, including *Which bee gives you a second chance? The Plan Bee.* The page included a drawing of a smiling bee, a love note to the hive, and a thank-you to its protectors.

That was the first few days. The notes multiplied over the next month. I found flowers laid in front of the hive as an offering and wondered if they'd been put there by a friend of mine, a fellow witch who lives in the neighborhood. I knew most of the residents who left notes probably didn't identify as nature worshippers or animists. Rather, the love they poured out to the bees came from the simple compassion that resides in all of us, even those of us indoctrinated by cultures of death, if we give kinship space to thrive. The notes were both a shield for the bees—what monster would plug up the hive in the midst of so much support?—and a balm for my heart.

Even so, I knew the hive's safety wasn't assured, and the truce was fragile. Sure enough, the following July, one year after the first attack, the hive was gassed and blocked again. Some bees survived, but the damage to the colony was brutal. Someone did some research and found out that years ago, the hive was mistakenly reported to the city as a hornet's nest, and it ended up on a yearly extermination schedule. (What monster would plug up the hive? The worst kind, apparently: a bureaucrat.) Someone posted notes with the names of city officials to contact. A few weeks later, a new note announced that the city didn't want to get sued if anyone was stung, so it wasn't going to back down.

Here's where the saga of the bees gets very weird. Someone found a beekeeper who was willing to move the hive. I didn't catch the whole process, but it was helpfully documented in a series of photos someone taped to the wall. The beekeeper lured the queen out through a big glass tube that he attached midway up the tree trunk. After that, her workers dutifully followed her into a temporary nest, and when the whole colony had been transferred, the beekeeper sealed up the hive entrance in the tree with chicken wire.

It was a happy ending, if a bittersweet one. We couldn't say hello to our bees anymore, but they were safe. They could thrive. One final note announced that the colony was now installed in its permanent home in Malibu.

Except it wasn't the final note. Months later, I passed by to find another note asking people not to remove the chicken wire, explaining that if a new colony moved in, those bees would be killed.

Why would someone take off the wire? I suspect that it was someone well-intentioned, someone who didn't know about the extermination schedule, or who thought that the nails holding the wire on were hurting the tree. Regardless of their intention, though, the damage was done. The entrance was exposed, and a new colony moved in. That July, right on schedule, the city came and destroyed it.

And the situation is even more complicated than I've let on so far. Honeybees aren't native to California or even the United States. Studies are starting to reveal that honeybees are impacting native bee populations, and the plants that rely on those native bees for pollination. But the impact of honeybees feels like a minor issue compared to the catastrophe staring us down all over the planet. The temperature climbs higher every year, the weather is more erratic, the wildfires and heat waves are increasingly out of control, and the people at the top of the hierarchy, those who have the most power to change course and do good, just can't stop killing.

Thinking about the bees, I find myself thinking again about Nancy from *The Craft*.

What if, when the girls in *The Craft* started manifesting their powers, everyone around them recognized them as priestesses instead of ostracizing them as witches? After all, the figure we now recognize as the witch is a kind of inverted priestess. An order of Melissai and a coven of witches are all avatars of mother goddesses, symbols of female power—only we distort that life-giving power through a dark filter that renders it demonic. What if Nancy had been recognized, elevated, and revered for her power? What if she'd been taken in by elders who could nurture and train her? It would have made for a pretty boring horror movie, but it's a poignant look at what our culture could have been.

Not that there aren't plenty of witches out there who are also contemporary priestesses. Sometimes, the label is a practical one, given to a practitioner by their community: someone who leads rituals, tends a shrine, or performs spiritual counseling. There are also, unfortunately, some self-aggrandizing witches who bestow the title upon themselves, hoping to cash in on the mystique. The internet teems with crystal priestesses and life coach priestesses and interdimensional cosmic ascension priestesses, many of whom have very good PR reps and very little training. Like the idea of a certified herbalist, the word *priestess* sometimes doesn't mean anything outside of marketing.

But maybe honeybees can help us figure out what an actual priestess can be. Maybe a priestess is someone who does the authentic, honest, and useful work needed most by the Earth. Maybe a priestess is someone who strives to learn the Earth's language so that they understand her when she tells them what action is needed and when. Maybe the true priestess fans their wings to protect her from heat and uses their sting against those who try to harm her. Becoming a Melissa isn't a threshold that a practitioner can cross with a ceremony and certificate. It's a lifelong path to which we can dedicate our imperfect, often failing selves.

In the camphor tree, where someone has torn out the mud that the city used to block the hive entrance, a few worker bees edge their way in and out. Inside the secret heartwood chambers, the survivors make their honey and tend to their brood and dream of an uncertain future. Within them and around them, the Goddess and the land dream, as well.

## A Spell to Turn Bitterness into Honey

Emerge from the womb of your dark place. Blink in the sunlight. Feel the threshold under your feet, the countless scents in the breeze, the glittering faceted world before you. Warm up your muscles. Depart.

This may terrify you, but you can explore in any direction you want. That means that you may travel in circles before you find what you're looking for. You may grow tired. You may have to double back and pass your home as you head in another direction—but you can't go inside to rest and eat, not yet, not until you've brought back your share of nourishment.

Seek out the flowers that are growing specifically for you, the ones that evolved just to call to you. Remember that they may not always be the sweetest ones. Some of them may be downright forbidding. You may have to brave poisons and predators. You may grow tattered and ragged. Why are the plants here so hostile, if they grew just for you? Why are there so many defenses up in this place? You may know the answer, or you may not. Just remember that your job is to look for the sweetness hidden in the bitterness. You may find yourself foraging in a garden of your own pain: all your heartbreak, sadness, disappointment, and discouragement blossoming in garish colors..Take a moment with each blossom you find. Explore it with your senses. Let the memories come.

How strange, that even in the midst of all that bitterness, there's still good, pure nectar to be found. Seek it out and drink it up. Don't be afraid—your body knows what to do with it.

Take it home to the Underworld, safe inside your own body. Take it into the deepest, most pitch-black place, the place you'll have to navigate by smell and feel. As you descend, a transformation will occur inside your body.

You have siblings in the Underworld with you. Can you find them? Listen for the hum of their movements, the vibration of their dances. You were never alone in this journey, even when you couldn't see your allies. Your siblings make art to call to you. You'll find your way to each other, dear heart. You'll get there.

Find them, recognize them, get to know them, and then look: Your honey is finished. It's been transformed into something rich and life-giving. Savor it, explore it, and then share it with your siblings. Share it with the young ones. Let them share their treasures with you in return. Teach others how to forage for goodness in bitter gardens.

Together, after you've all drunk your fill, journey back into the light. There's so much pain out there, so many wrongs that need righting. The flowers of the field are waiting for you, so go find them.

# 10

## Incantation

### On timeline jumping, the multiverse, and the voice as a magical tool

### Lesson 1: Body

One day, hearing a song I liked on the radio after dropping the kids off at school, I noticed that my singing voice had disappeared. When I was young, I sang in the shower, in the car, and around the house while I did chores. Back in high school and college I'd been a soloist, singing in a capella groups and a barbershop quartet. That day in the car, though, I realized I physically couldn't hold a note anymore. No matter how much I strained, my voice went flat, like a guitar peg working itself loose. How long had it been since I'd sung to myself, just for the pleasure of it?

If our voices are formed by the topography of our insides, the way our muscles and vocal folds work to produce sound, then what did my voice say about me? That I was a powerful woman who could shape air into beauty? Or that I was a tired, middle-aged mother of two, with my core muscles still sagging from pregnancy and my throat tight with the stress of childcare? Most mornings, I woke up with worry lines from frowning in my sleep. I didn't work out anymore. My body felt like a mess.

I'd heard, here and there, about people taking voice lessons. Not professional singers, not even people with particularly good voices, but just normal folks who wanted to sing a little better around campfires. After many weeks of privately testing my voice, trying and failing to reach high notes and hold steady tones, it occurred to me that I could take voice lessons, too. Could a voice teacher help me troubleshoot why my voice had left me? I tossed out the idea to my husband one day, and the worst possible thing happened: He took me seriously. He signed me up for a package of four lessons as a birthday present. Now I actually had to go through with it.

My teacher's name was Anastasia. The Omicron variant of COVID was surging, and I was afraid of infecting someone by breathing inside their home, but we were both vaccinated, so I took off my mask and fidgeted by the weathered piano in the corner of her studio apartment. Anastasia was a young opera singer who was a thousand times prettier than me, but with her glasses and wide smile, she was disarmingly sweet. "Let's start with some stretches," she said, as if we were at the gym.

We touched our toes and bent our arms back and tilted our heads from side to side. I never did this in high school choir. As we stretched, she explained the physiology of the voice. "Your lungs are your bellows," she said, "but you don't have to blast a lot of air to get volume. Instead, you want to make the sound resonate in your head. Open up your mouth like you're yawning—feel that space behind your soft palate? That chamber is like the inside of a violin. Lift your head off your jaw." Lift my head off my jaw? It was the kind of yoga studio instruction that shouldn't make any sense but somehow does. I imagined my head floating off my jaw, and I thought I felt some space open up between my nose and my throat.

When we sing, Anastasia explained, we play an instrument that we can't see: an instrument as complex as a guitar or a piano, but stitched to our interiors with fascia and sinew, so that we can only access it by feel. I thought of my own hidden channels and hollows, dull and weak from disuse, the secret landscape that had become as foreign as another planet to me. Anastasia had me sing scales, and I cringed at the pinched little wheeze that came out.

"You sound great," she said kindly. At the end of the lesson, she asked what my goal was.

What *was* my goal? Why was I here, wasting our money and ignoring my children? Sometimes I felt like my witch fire had gone out. Every moment was devoted to either my job or the kids. When I was younger, I had waking visions and precognitive dreams. Gods had spoken to me. Magic had worked. Now, a year into my forties, I felt like my whole life had gone off the rails. I hated my job, but I didn't know how to find a new one. Between COVID and climate change, it felt like there was no past and no future, only the static present of waiting for disaster. I longed to delight in myself again.

"I like doing karaoke," I said, but even that was kind of a lie. Karaoke wasn't fun unless I was drunk.

"Bring a song to work on at our next lesson," Anastasia said.

## Lesson 2: Breath

"Singing is magic," writes Nancy Marie Brown in *The Real Valkyrie*, her study of Viking women. "To hold a room in thrall, a singer out-matches her audience. She pulls the song from her enormous heart and aims it at each of their little hearts. She inhales all the air in the room and sings it out, altered. . . . If you sing something—if you say something—it becomes real." Brown points out that the word *seiðr*, in Old Norse, means both "witchcraft" and "song."

If you take a class in witchcraft, or study under a teacher, breathing may be one of your first lessons. As in yoga and meditation, the breath is one of the witch's most fundamental tools, the practice that gives rise to all other forms of magic. You breathe to ground yourself in your body, to slow your heartbeat and calm your limbic system. You breathe to take in what some witches call "virtue"—the hum of life all around you, the fire that flows in the arteries of the Earth—and then invite it to rise into your bloodstream, so you can channel it into your rites and incantations. With your breath, you take in the air that the trees have exhaled, turn it into $CO_2$ and then send it back out for the trees to inhale again. Breathing is an act of connection with everything around you, a web that tethers you to all other life.

But breathing hadn't been easy for me lately. In the first few weeks of the pandemic, when everyone knew the virus was swirling around in the air and no one wore any protection, I sewed masks out of an old pillowcase and people at the supermarket stared at me. One day, after the library reopened for curbside service, a woman showed up with a hacking cough and no mask and asked me to lean over her phone with her to look for something in the catalog. I eventually got my hands on an N95 and started using it not just for COVID, but for wildfire smoke. I took to holding my breath whenever I passed another person on the street, whether they were masked or not. Breathing was fraught and dangerous, an opening for death to swoop in.

At my second lesson, Anastasia told me to blow a raspberry with my lips while humming a couple of notes. In high school choir we made all sorts of ridiculous noises during our daily warm-ups—sirens and buzzes and hisses and nonsense syllables—but I still giggled as I tried to do it in Anastasia's living room. It's one thing to blow raspberries as a singer in a group of thirty other singers blowing raspberries. It's quite another to do it by yourself, old and out of practice, with no performance to prepare for and a teacher staring at you. I couldn't get more than one note out before I lost my air. "Again," Anastasia said. I tried again and again, but my lungs kept collapsing partway through.

Anastasia frowned, and I could tell she didn't have a diagnosis. She ran me through some scales and those sounded terrible, too.

I wished she could hear how I sounded when I was young. At one high school concert, I sang Janis Joplin's "Mercedes Benz," and by the end of the first verse, the whole audience was clapping along. People came up to me afterward and told me they'd never known I had such a great voice, I was usually so quiet. Back then, I'd had space to let my voice rip free from my body. I'd had microphones and cavernous auditoriums to amplify it, hours a day set aside just for my voice.

"Let me hear your song," Anastasia said.

It was a song I'd first heard ten years before, when I spent a summer studying Yiddish in Lithuania. It was one of my favorite Yiddish folk songs:

Hob ich mir a shpan, gedekt mit shvartzn leder
Un tzvey leiben ferd, un fir reder
Un di reder dreyen nit, un di ferd geyen nit
Un dos vaib zi shilt zich, un a glezel bronfin vilt zich
Ze ich mir a shteyn, zitz ich mir un veyn

The words translate to "I have a carriage lined with black leather, and four wheels, and two fine horses. But the wheels won't turn, and the horses won't go, and my wife is complaining, and I want a little whiskey. I see a stone, so I sit on it and weep." The song goes on to describe all the lives the singer would have lived if he'd only had the tools. "I would have been a cobbler," he sings, "but I don't have an awl; I would have been a cantor, but I don't have a voice." I've only ever heard one grainy recording of the song, in an online archive for Yiddish music. It's eerie in its melancholy, the ghost of a life wasted a century ago.

My ancestors were pessimists, running from pogroms and political upheaval, carving out new lives for themselves while always waiting for the other shoe to drop. Witches, nowadays, are supposed to be militant optimists. We're supposed to be the ones manifesting everything we want and then posting it on glittery social media accounts. But all the witches I know in real life are dealing with the same problems as everyone else. No one can afford a good home. Everyone's worried about money. These struggles are why, throughout history, people have come to folk magic and witchcraft in the first place: because the world doesn't hand us things just because we desperately need them.

I tried to put some feeling into the song as I sang it for Anastasia, but neither of us could hear me over her piano. I tried to lift my head off my jaw and play my hidden instrument. In the back of my mind, I felt the dread of going to work the next day, of dealing with aggressive patrons and a petulant boss. I wanted to quit and walk away forever, but I'd been a librarian for ten years and I didn't know how to do anything else. What other job could I possibly get?

"*Hob ich mir a shpan*," I sang. The song sounded so bleak when I sang it out loud. If only I had an awl, if only I had a voice, if only, if only, if only.

## Lesson 3: Tone

The next week, Anastasia was shaken when she let me in. "My neighbors just banged on the wall," she said. "I was giving a piano lesson to a kid and they banged on it! Quiet hours don't start until 10 and I already told them I wouldn't give lessons after 7! I don't know what they want from me!"

Apparently, her neighbors complained about her lessons all the time. I asked if I should come back another day, and she said no, it was fine, if the neighbors banged again she'd go over and talk to them. But I could hear the fear in her voice, and I instantly recognized the kind of neighbor she had, because I'd had that kind of neighbor, too. When my older kid was a newborn, our downstairs neighbor had complained about our footsteps in the middle of the night. We'd worn socks and tiptoed, but nothing helped. These days, I didn't like drawing attention to myself if I could help it. I'd had more than one relative snipe at me for doing things that were supposedly a distraction from mothering, like reading books and making art. Now that I was a mother, my own personhood had to be kept secret.

Anastasia and I did our usual stretches and breathing exercises. I still couldn't do that damn raspberry. When I sang scales, though, Anastasia beamed when my voice finally gave out. "Look how high you went!" she said. "You made it up to a D!" I smiled, but all I could think about were her faceless neighbors, hunched on the other side of the wall with a broom handle in their talons, fuming over the space I was taking up.

The voice allows us to bring the unseen to light, to make real and even tangible the secret calculations of our synapses and neurons. Just as the breath binds us to the world around us, the voice allows us to manipulate it. The song, the scream, the ballad, the whisper, the laugh—they all shape our worlds. In the Bible, God creates the universe with a word. In the Finnish epic the Kalavala, the hero Väinämöinen defeats his enemies by singing at them. One of the most pivotal acts of the Morrigan is a prophecy she chants on the battlefield at Moytura, singing a song of peace and abundance that decays into ruin. Science-fiction writer Ted Chiang writes that ancient Pythagoreans chanted vowels to draw power from the heavens because "the sounds we make are simultaneously our intentions and our life force." Look at any grimoire and you'll see the primacy of incantation in magic and ritual. When we navigate our way through a hostile place, struggling to find space for our bodies and minds, every buzz of our vocal folds is a spell.

At least, that's what it felt like as I sang in Anastasia's home, trying to give shape to my inner self, even as I dreaded being yelled at for it.

Over the years, as I've studied witchcraft in books and classes, I've seen magic described again and again as the art of leaving one path and stepping onto a new one. Witches traditionally practice magic at crossroads, where new paths can be taken. Some witches describe magic in terms of jumping timelines or switching train tracks. Writing about tarot as a method of creating a new future instead of just predicting it, tarotist Charlie Claire Burgess offers a vivid analogy: "Picture life as a cart rolling down a hill: the cart has momentum and inertia, and without guidance it will keep rolling in the direction that gravity sent it, for better or for worse. . . . Instead of placidly rolling downhill, we can use tarot to become aware of what needs our attention, decide to do something about it, and redirect our trajectory."

In other words, when you read the cards or pray to God or work a spell or make a vision board, you wrest yourself off your current track and hop onto a new one. A new timeline. A new life.

I'd started looking for a new job, poking around on this and that website, but my path as a librarian still felt as well-worn as a holloway. How was I going to jump tracks now? Despite my doubts, I started whispering affirmations each night before bed: *I have a new job that I love, I have a new job that I love, I have a new job that I love.* Standing at my altar before my roebuck skull, I was careful to phrase my wish as if it had already happened. Many witches will tell you that saying "I want" when working magic reinforces your sense of lacking something, instead of manifesting the thing itself. To effectively jump timelines, you have to trust that you're already in the new one, that the actions you're taking now have rippled backward to alter your past. To change your life requires the same beautifully foolish arrogance that lets you blast sound out of your mouth and trust that people want to hear it.

In Anastasia's living room, I sang "Hob Ich Mir a Shpan," trying to make it sound melancholy instead of just clumsy. I had practiced it all week, quietly after the kids had gone to bed, but I still didn't sound any better. I indulged in a depressing thought: If the narrator in the song got his awl, would he really become a cobbler? Or would the universe sweep the chance away from him in some other way?

Anastasia told me she still couldn't hear me over the piano. But your neighbors! I thought. Still, I did my best to be heard. My voice has no vibrato, and on one note I tried to fake it by wiggling my trachea. She saw through the trick instantly and told me to start again. *Volt ich geven a zinger,* I thought, *hob ich nit keyn* vibrato: I would have been a singer but I don't have any vibrato. I sang and sang and sang, moving that air, shaping those vowels, trying to turn my body into an instrument.

By the end, I wanted to crawl into a hole, but Anastasia seemed hopeful. "You're getting better," she said. "I can hear it. Your tone is getting stronger; you're hitting higher notes." My throat and soft palate felt tired and raw, but I nodded as I drank from my water bottle. I decided to believe her. As I walked home, I sang softly to myself, stopping whenever someone passed, holding my breath when I smelled dog poop, trying to hear in my voice a return to what I once loved. After the kids were in bed that night, I found a job listing for a freelance journalist. The pay wasn't enough to live on, so I'd have to do it on top of my library job. But I was qualified. Maybe it was a lever to start switching those rusty tracks.

The next morning, my older kid woke up coughing.

## Lesson 4: Song

Her COVID test was positive, and for a couple of minutes, amid the chaos of getting ready for the day, I was the only one who knew it. I stood over the test in the bathroom and began to laugh. I raked my hands through my hair, doubled over in unhinged, despairing laughter, and waited for it to turn into tears. After two years, COVID had found us. We couldn't hide forever.

We went into quarantine. For the next two weeks, my family and I were trapped with each other in our cluttered little home, where the virus picked us off one by one. My older kid was miserable for two days, moaning and coughing on the couch as *Pokémon* cartoons played on repeat. Just as she began to feel better, my symptoms emerged.

It started with a thickness in my throat, right where Anastasia had been telling me to open my soft palate. I spent the evening swallowing and swallowing, telling myself the air was dusty, I was thirsty, it was just my imagination. By the next morning, I was a shivering wreck, and I spent forty-eight hours in a feverish half-sleep as the vaccine fought the virus off. Whenever I woke up, I could feel all the progress in my voice falling away as my throat tore itself apart.

Maybe, I thought, this was one of those points where a new timeline could have branched, one in which my voice lessons led to something and I finally got the life I wanted. I'd left so many potential timelines in my wake. I'd only become a librarian because writing novels hadn't worked out. What if I'd done something more adventurous instead? What if I'd stuck with singing and gotten really good at it? Plenty of singers don't have vibrato and they sound great. What if

I'd studied acting in college, as I'd once planned to? What if I'd had a better math teacher in elementary school and I'd become a scientist? What if I'd focused on my art instead of having kids? That last time-line was a dark one that I didn't want to think about. I'd always wanted kids. They were my treasures. I didn't like feeling Lilith clawing at me, just as she had clawed at my mother.

I'd noticed that people had started talking about timelines an awful lot over the past few years. On election night in 2016, I went upstairs to give our kid her bath while Hillary Clinton raked in votes. When I came back down, my husband was pacing the living room and Trump was suddenly winning. Did I somehow break the universe during that twenty-minute bath? If it was me who landed us in the worst timeline, I'm sorry.

Since Trump's election, pop culture has been obsessed with time-lines, too. The multiverse is a very old trope in speculative fiction, but as I write this, it's having a moment. Is it cultural regret about climate change? Disgust at the rotting American empire? Millennial grief at how disappointing our lives turned out to be? Maybe. All I know is that the multiverse is everywhere these days. There's Loki, of course, hopping timelines with the TVA and meeting all his variants. Loki is just one chapter in Marvel's Multiverse Saga, in which Marvel heroes duke it out with alternate versions of themselves. After watching Loki, I came upon Ted Chiang's "Anxiety Is the Dizziness of Free-dom," a story in which people can talk to their other selves through a special kind of laptop. Then there's the film *Everything Everywhere All at Once*, which tells the story of a laundromat owner named Eve-lyn whose other self invented multiversal travel. In one of the most fascinating scenes, Evelyn finds out she could have been a famous singer—but only if she'd been blinded in childhood.

During my fever, I found myself getting bizarrely theoretical about the multiverse. Maybe, I thought, when you work magic and switch your tracks, you actually create another you in a different timeline. Maybe all the work I'd done in this life fed other selves who reaped the rewards. Why couldn't they all do some magic to help me in return? I knew the answer: It was because their lives were good enough that doing spellwork didn't occur to them.

I woke up a little. What on Earth? What a strange train of thought. I went back to sleep.

The virus ran its course, and eventually we all tested negative. During our quarantine, Los Angeles County dropped its mask mandate, and we reemerged into a world that was suddenly maskless and carefree. Maybe I broke the universe again. When I went back for my final lesson with Anastasia, I worried out loud that I was still contagious, but she waved it off. It turned out she'd had the COVID Omicron variant months before.

After the two weeks of illness and missed practice, my voice was back at square one. I croaked out some scales, failed at the raspberry again, and groaned inside when Anastasia said it was time to move on to "Hob Ich Mir a Shpan." Back in Lithuania, when I'd first learned the song, I'd fallen in love with the haunting melody, the strange yet relatable story. Now I was sick of it. I was sick of the carriage. I was sick of the poor loser and his awl. I never wanted to sing it again. I never wanted to sing anything again.

But this was my last lesson, and it was half over, so this was my last chance.

Once, at a choir concert, I was fretting backstage when an older singer gave me some advice. "Sing from the place where you're only singing for yourself," she said. "Don't worry about the audience. Even when you're in front of people, just sing for yourself." I nailed that solo, so I tried the same thing now. I closed my eyes and sang for myself.

My voice was drowned out by the piano. Anastasia couldn't hear me at all.

But when our time ran out and I edged toward my purse, she seemed to have an epiphany. "I think I know what your problem is," she said.

I paused.

"Just sing louder." I must have made a face, because she laughed. "I think that's literally your only problem," she said. "You're holding back. You're just not singing loud enough. Sing louder."

I thought of the years I'd spent with children sleeping in the next room, neighbors on the other side of my walls. I thought of all the years I'd spent hiding myself away, trudging down a path others expected of me, dreaming of other lives. Didn't Anastasia understand? I couldn't sing louder. If I sang louder, people would hear me.

I walked home, holding my breath as I passed the usual dog poop, finally letting out a post-COVID cough I'd been holding in for an hour. But when I got to the front door of my building, my timeline diverged. Instead of going inside, I went down to the garage.

Usually at this time of night, the garage was full of people coming home from work, but tonight it was empty—and the acoustics, I happened to know, were incredible. Sing louder? Really? That was the solution? Someone would probably come in at any second, so I didn't have long to try.

"Hob ich mir a shpan," I sang, "gedekt in shvartzn leder." I filled my lungs and made the next line a little louder. "Un tzvey leiben ferd, un fir reder." No one could hear me. I was all alone. I sang for myself, louder and louder, until my voice echoed off the walls.

Soon I found a place I thought I'd forgotten: a place I reached when I was young, singing onstage or in the car or under the shower spray. I sang for myself. I would have been a merchant, but I don't have any merchandise. I would have been a wise man, but I don't have any wisdom. The song was a cry to the heavens, a fervent rune, a desperate spell. I would have been so much more if things had gone differently. I could have been so much more. I could be so much more. Help me be more.

Later, when I checked my email before bed, I would find an interview request for the freelance job. An opening. The squeak of slowly shifting tracks.

But right then, in the garage, I sang until I thought I felt it: a small space in the multiverse that belonged only to me, the hum of magic shaping itself into my incantation. Or maybe it was yet another timeline shooting away from me, one that I would never even see.

## A Spell to Find Your Crossroads

It may seem like your path is laid out before you: straight, unending, with no turnoffs or exits. But someone out there benefits from your belief that you have no other options, and it's worth it to ask yourself who. You don't have to judge them. They may not even realize what they're doing. Just take a moment to notice. That's the first step in finding your crossroads.

It also may be tempting to try to find your crossroads by continuing to walk forward. After all, if you'd already come upon the path you wanted, you would have taken it! But notice the trap you've just fallen into: again, you're telling yourself that the only way to go is forward. That just isn't true.

So before you make another move, just pause. Stop walking. Take a breath, relax, sit down, and have a snack. Drink some water from your flask and wipe the sweat from your brow. Make a fire if it's chilly, or take off a layer if it's hot. Notice the friendly weeds who grow along the side of the road. Don't worry, you've got some time to think. You don't have to race toward the end of your life.

As you relax, you may start to notice how much fear you're carrying with you. It sticks to the inside of you, gumming up your voice, stiffening your limbs. Fear doesn't open up new paths—it closes them off. That won't do at all! Feel around in your pockets and you'll find a container. You may pull out a small vial, holding barely more than a dram; you may miraculously heft a sloshing bucket out of your coat. Hold your vessel, swirl it around, and take a sniff of the liquid inside. This is the stuff that will cleanse you of your fear.

How you use it is up to you. Maybe it's meant to be taken internally, like medicine, like a singer's cup of tea with honey before a concert. Or maybe you apply it externally, like a hot shower. I'll give you a moment to figure it out. Do it whenever you're ready.

There, isn't that better? Now look around you.

Did you have any idea that you were standing at a crossroads this entire time? Be honest. The truth is, we carry crossroads with us wherever we go, and we never think to set foot on them.

And there's an especially funny thing about this particular junction. The more you look at it, the more branches it seems to grow. It starts off with four: the road you're on, and another one bisecting it. But soon there seem to be eight, then a hundred, and then infinite paths branching out like chrysanthemum petals. All you have to do is choose one.

No pressure, right?

It's okay. You don't have to see to the end of every path to make your choice. In fact, you can't. Some paths will look like they're filled with jagged rocks. Some will be shrouded in fog. Beware the paths that look suspiciously easy, a little too cheerful and verdant. If you turn in a circle, you'll see a dizzying variety of different roads you can take.

So how do you choose? Here's a little trick I picked up. Open your mouth and sing. A sacred chant, a folk tune, a pop song, it doesn't matter. Sing whatever brings you joy, whatever feels good in your throat and inviting on your tongue. Sing, and listen for the path that answers.

When you hear your own voice echoing back to you, stronger and more certain than an echo has ever sounded—almost as if your future self is calling back to you and saying, *Yes, this is the way. Come on. You're almost there!*—you'll know you've found the path to take.

And if something goes sideways? If it turns out that the future isn't written in stone and an avalanche buries the road or an earthquake opens up a crevasse? Well, you'll always have your vessel, your crossroads, and your voice. If the time comes to choose a new path again, you'll know what to do.

# 11

# We Can All Be Arks

## How to pass on a legacy
## through seed and soil

I'd always wanted a cottage in the woods. But when we outgrew our apartment, I realized I'd have to settle for a condo with an alley.

It was 2017 and the housing market was already spiraling, but we found a run-down building filled with retirees. When we went to look at the unit for sale, we discovered that it was the only one in the building with a kitchen door leading out to a tiny porch. In a corner behind the building was a cramped ficus tree, no doubt some decades-old bad landscaping decision, and my older daughter promptly started to climb its mountainous roots. That was how I knew we would live here: There was a little bit of land, and my child had made friends with it. There weren't any plants, but there was room for some. This could work.

Plus, our other option was a condo sandwiched between the freeway and a gas station.

While she climbed the tree, I wandered the alley to look at the soil, which was compacted and rocky and covered in garbage. Developers commonly scrape away topsoil when they build; where that topsoil goes—that soil that may have been millennia in the making—I'm not sure. The land was hurting, its surface a raw abrasion, but maybe I could help. I was losing hope that I'd ever have the lush permaculture garden I'd always imagined, with grapevine canopies and twisting rows of witching herbs. My husband's job was here in LA, and he wasn't leaving it anytime soon. Maybe I'd have a garden of my own when we retired. At least this building came with a little earth that no one seemed to care about.

We made an offer and the owner accepted it suspiciously quickly. In fact, she didn't even sell it for what she was asking. Our realtor made a typo in the dollar amount, and that mistake accidentally got us a $10,000 discount. The owner either didn't notice the mistake or was so desperate to get rid of the place that she didn't care.

While we were unpacking, we heard a knock at the door. I opened it to find an ancient woman in a nightshirt and slippers. "I'm with the board," she said, pushing her way past me into our new home. "I'm here to tell you about the rules."

The board: the Homeowners' Association board of directors. HOAs, if you've been fortunate enough never to deal with one, are the groups of residents that govern places like condominiums and gated communities. In a condo building, someone has to be responsible for fixing cracks and leaks in the building, so I understood the basic concept. I just hadn't known that HOAs involved people forcing their way into your living room in their pajamas.

The board member shuffled around, rattling off a litany of obscure-sounding rules as she looked in our boxes and peered around corners. Finally, she got to the patio outside our living room and looked out. She waved at some paint cans the previous owner had left behind. "You can't have those there," she said.

I ignored the fact that the cans had sat there for months, unnoticed. "I was thinking about putting some plants out in the alley," I said. "Next to the path."

"Not allowed," she barked, and left.

Say the word *gardener* in Southern California, and you'll evoke a truck full of blades: lawnmowers, weed whackers, and power saws. A gardener, in this place, isn't someone who nurtures life and encourages growth. A gardener is someone who cuts and slices and hacks at plants, forcing them into submission. A gardener is someone who goes door to door with a gas-powered leaf blower, filling the air with its roar as they stuff leaves that could have turned into soil into trash bags. A gardener is a low-wage worker, often an immigrant, who would probably rather be planting things. A gardener is someone who's ordered to kill, eradicate, and destroy.

In California, gardeners and HOAs go hand in hand, and over the next few months, I discovered just how bonkers HOAs really are. My sister came to see the place, and a board member screamed at her for bringing her stroller through the front lobby instead of the garage. All the bikes in the garage were stolen, but when a few of us tucked our bikes behind the stairwell, another board member ordered the locks cut and the bikes hauled away. "They're ugly!" she fumed, shaking her head at the handlebars poking out from behind the peeling paint on the industrial staircase. Typewritten index cards periodically appeared on the garage bulletin board, scolding people for leaving furniture on the curb when it wasn't bulky trash day. When we finally had the money to buy a place, I'd celebrated not having a landlord anymore. Now I had thirty-three of them.

But I still wanted to plant things. At first, I tried doing it surreptitiously. After all, the back alley was full of trash—if everyone was okay with that, what problem could they possibly have with some plants? Plus, someone had clearly done a little gardening before me, installing a flowerless rosebush right in the middle of the path. But the day after I planted some seeds and lined the space with the paving stones that were scattered across the alley, someone came by and kicked it to pieces. I went on the internet and found people who'd been fined by their HOAs for planting flowers. I found one horror story about a guy whose HOA had foreclosed on his house. What the hell was wrong with these people? Out of the infinite leisure activities a human being has to choose from, this was how they spent their time?

If only, I found myself thinking, my neighbors could see things through the eyes of a gardener. I mean the real kind of gardener, the kind who grows things. My husband and I had taken a native plant gardening class after we bought the condo, sitting with thirty other gardeners in a little classroom with no A/C, taking notes as the teacher described plant communities and design principles. We studied photo after photo of sprawling gardens, bursting with ceanothus bushes and poppy beds. It was a far cry from the landscaping in the front of our building, which held only the usual lawn and palm trees. For most of the class, I happily geeked out over pollinators and live oak species, but near the end, things suddenly turned profound.

Gardeners plant native species even in the midst of climate change, we learned, not because they plan to keep those species on life support forever, but because they hope that someday the plants will be able to flourish on their own again. If you save the plants, you save all the animals that evolved alongside those plants and depend on them: Insects, songbirds, predators, entire ecosystems. We learned that under the care of a skilled gardener, even a small yard can be an ark.

An ark. I liked that.

That analogy refers to Noah's ark, of course, but stories of devastating floods can be found in mythologies all over the world, a specter of apocalypse that haunts our collective psyche, a warning whispered by the gods. In the *Epic of Gilgamesh*, a group of gods decide to destroy the world, but Ea, "the cleverest of the gods," warns Noah's Akkadian counterpart Utnapishtim of the destruction that's coming. Ea whispers through the reed walls of Utnapishtim's home:

> You reed house walls, listen and hear me whisper;
> listen and be attentive to what I tell you.
> Utnapishtim, son of Ubartutu,
> abandon your house, abandon what you possess,
> abandon your house and build a boat instead.
> Seek life instead of riches, save yourself.
> Take with you, on the boat you build, an instance
> of each thing living so that they may be
> safe from obliteration in the flood.

In this version of the flood myth, the gods aren't unanimous in their decision to destroy humanity. In fact, they quickly come to regret it, "cringing against the wall [of Heaven] like beaten dogs" to escape the rising water. To me, this version of the story feels closer to the reality of climate change than the Noah myth does. After all, God in the Noah myth has a long-term plan, if a heartless one, and God makes sure there are survivors afterward. The gods in *Gilgamesh* think they're above the coming disaster, and only realize too late that they happen to live in the world they're destroying.

A dark thing happens to people's minds when they live long enough under industrial capitalism, which sees nothing as sacred except manufactured wealth. They begin to hold life itself in contempt, seeing other organisms not as partners and neighbors, but as competitors and threats. They see a bee pollinating their flowers, or a datura plant in blossom, as an enemy to be conquered. They get used to monocultures and conformity, and balk at the sight of an untrimmed hedge. They forget how to be a community. The flood myth is happening all around us, right now. There are literal floods happening all over the world—and droughts and famines and hurricanes and wildfires—but at the root of them all is an ideology that's killing us.

But we can be arks, I thought. On the first full moon after we moved in, I brought my ritual supplies to the roof of the building to perform an esbat in our new home. Not for the first time, I found a part of myself preparing to instruct my daughters in witchcraft when they came of age, if they wanted it. "This is how you'll explain the witch's compass," a little voice said as I conjured the quarter spirits. "This is how you'll teach reverence for life," it murmured as I held my hands up to the moon. Then I thought, *Maybe I'm an ark.* My body, my mind, my knowledge, the traditions I've stored up inside of me. I carry them through the years so that I can pass them on and so that their recipients can pass them on, and so on until the danger has passed.

Faced with an anonymous army of cranky neighbors, I did the only thing I could think of: I joined the HOA board.

. After the election, there were four of us on the new board, and we each had our own agenda. One joined because she wanted a second parking spot in the garage. Another—the one who had had people's bikes taken away—wanted an easy way to tattle on all her neighbors. The third wanted the board to stop paying for "frivolous" repairs like burst pipes and mold remediation. Then there was me, with my determination to plant native shrubs. If our interests had been at all aligned, we would have made a proper coven.

Luckily, as soon as I was a board member, everyone accepted my proposal as perfectly reasonable. I took a landscaping class, bought a pile of books, and drafted a plan on graph paper. I made up little signs saying the garden was HOA approved. It seems people will let you do whatever you want as long as you tell them you're in charge. It's part of the reason human civilization has gotten itself into this mess, but a savvy witch uses all the tools at their disposal.

I went to the nursery and picked out some plants. The lighting was tricky, with the sun disappearing behind the building all winter, so I had to choose carefully. I got California fuschia, which has firecracker-red flowers in spring that hummingbirds love. I got sagebrush, an aromatic artemisia related to mugwort, and milkweed for monarch butterflies. I got a Cleveland sage plant—the same plant one of my witchcraft teachers had always brought to class with her, arranging cuttings on the altar and filling the room with dusky perfume. I knew the sage wouldn't like the clay soil, so I got her a pot, and I bought a packet of California poppy seeds to scatter along the side of the path. After a good rain, I put everything in. I feared that the soil was just too bad for them to survive, but as I dug, I noticed it was teeming with earthworms. The land was impatient to be healed.

The problem with California native plants is that they don't look ornamental compared to the imported tropicals that people tend to use in landscaping. One of the books I bought, *California Native Plants for the Garden*, explains why developers are so intent on ripping out native plants: "Compared to the rich greens, bright flowers, and bold textures of subtropical species," the authors write, "the natives must have seemed dull and gray." But plumeria and hibiscus, as gorgeous as they are, suffer in this dry climate. Native plants were made for it.

Would the plants just look like overgrown weeds to be hacked away? I fretted about that, but then I reminded myself of all the trash I'd cleaned up to make room for them. No one cared. Plus, the HOA signs were like protective talismans.

After you put plants in the ground, there's a tense period in which you wait to see if they'll take root or not. Sometimes plants just don't thrive, no matter how perfectly matched for the space they are. The plants that make it, though, will usually sit there for a while, and then suddenly experience a burst of new growth when their root systems take hold. Seeing all those new buds appear is an indescribable feeling for a gardener. For a few weeks, I anxiously waited to see which plants would grow and which would wither.

Some of the smaller plants died. Only a few of the poppies sprouted. But the roots of the fuschia, sagebrush, and sage caught. They quickly grew into big, happy shrubs, and, in the spring, they bloomed. Hummingbirds and butterflies flocked to the red and purple flowers. I found monarch caterpillars on the milkweed, and even spotted a giant swallowtail. I began to notice more birds' nests in the surrounding trees. I pruned the sagebrush back every few months, keeping the cuttings as incense. I arranged sage branches on my altar just as my teacher had done. People stopped littering in the alley. I began to spend my mornings on the back porch, sipping coffee among the plants and feeling the presence of the Good Folk around me.

It felt like my own secret garden, my own little ark. Not only that, but the plants had had a ripple effect on the space around them, making the entire alley greener and healthier. I don't claim to be an expert gardener or landscaper—what I did, anyone can do—but every time I looked out at the butterflies and hummingbirds from my kitchen window, I thought, *I did that. I made that happen.*

On the surface, gardening may seem like a paltry, even indulgent form of activism. But nurturing threatened species requires radical hope, which philosopher Jonathan Lear defines as hope that's "directed toward a future goodness that transcends the current ability to understand what it is." The act of planting keeps despair at bay. Even if a plant doesn't live long, it may release a seed that flies somewhere safe and carries the species forward. Besides, liberation becomes easier to imagine when you get a glimpse of what lies on the other side. Looking at a healthy garden, your body remembers a future with gardens, and that promise propels you to action.

And once you have a garden, you realize that arks can come in many forms. A plant, a song, a fable, a ritual, a tradition: anything can be an ark.

Pop culture, for instance, can be an ark for something ancient and important. Actually, I'd argue that pop culture can be an especially durable ark. Grimoires or tomes of folklore aren't always page-turners, but a coven of witches invoking Manon on the beach can teach a theater full of teens how to perform an invocation. A comic book super-villain can be a vehicle for a god craving adoration while he weathers a dry spell, when people can't hear the songs of gods. A movie about the multiverse can give us the vocabulary we need to imagine endless possibilities—and then try to sing a better reality into being. Witchcraft lives everywhere, hiding in all the countless seams and stitches of the world.

A new guy moved into the building, a TV producer used to being in charge, and as soon as the board election rolled around, he got himself elected president. Meanwhile, exhausted from all the non-gardening duties that had come with keeping a thirty-four-unit building from collapsing into rubble, I stepped down. After all, I figured, the garden was thriving, and my work was done.

One day, about three years after I planted the garden, I ran an errand and came home through the back alley. I was lost in thought, staring at the ground in front of me as I walked, so I didn't notice what was wrong until I was upon it. The garden was gone, with bare dirt in its place.

For a minute I just stared, trying to process what I was seeing. There was nothing left. The soil had been raked, or more likely blasted with a leaf blower, so that there wasn't a single twig remaining. The ground was already crisping in the sun. Even the potted sage had been torn out by the roots, the empty pot left sitting by the wall. I stumbled inside, where I began to sob.

I emailed the board, and the new president wasted no time in laying into me. The plants in the alley had been removed, he told me, because their thorns were scratching people. *What?* I thought. *What thorns?* Then I realized he had to be talking about the rosebush in the middle of the path, the one that had been there when I moved in, and had snagged my clothes more than once. Someone must have complained about it, and he must have told the gardeners to just get rid of everything. I told him that none of the native plants had had thorns, and I had been keeping them neatly pruned anyway, and at the suggestion that maybe he had made a mistake, he went on offense. Were those more plants on my patio? Did I have permission for those? Maybe he should look into it, he told me. Maybe he should call me into a hearing. If he ever caught me planting stuff again, I'd be fined.

For a while after that, I couldn't bring myself to garden. There's no feeling in the world like watching the cotyledons of a sprouting seed unfurl, or seeing the first hint of a flower bud at the tip of a stem, but I lost all interest. When the plants in my window boxes succumbed to that year's heat wave, I didn't bother to replace them. None of the neighbors seemed to notice the brown husks in my window boxes. The alley soon filled with trash again. I lived as a condo owner in Los Angeles is expected to live: with the curtains drawn and the A/C going.

I didn't expect anyone to understand my grief at the lost garden, but people did. They understood. Friends reached out; my husband promised that someday I'd have land of my own to tend. There are still people out there, even people who don't garden themselves, who understand that a garden is a sacred thing. That means there's hope for us.

There was one plant left after the slaughter. It was a golden currant shrub that I'd planted on the other side of the building. The gardeners must not have been ordered to do that side, because none of the plants there had been touched. The golden currant had taken a long time to get established, fighting the roots of the ficus tree in the corner, and it had never flowered or fruited. One day, though, I noticed yellow buds.

I slowly returned to gardening. I replaced the plants in my window boxes with fresh seedlings. I stubbornly kept going to the roof for esbats, stepping lightly so that no one would hear me. The HOA president was running amok, fining people left and right for walking too loudly or splashing in the pool, and I worked a spell to get rid of him. I'll state for the record that this next part was pure coincidence: Soon after my spell, he fell out of favor with the membership and moved out of the building not long after that. A hummingbird made a nest in a tree outside my window and hatched two chicks.

The buds on the golden currant tree grew into flowers, and those flowers swelled into currants. The fruit, like the flowers, was red like blood and yellow like fire. One evening, I picked some of them, leaving others for the birds, and brought my tiny harvest inside to share with my daughters. As we sat around the table and savored the tangy sweetness on our tongues, I imagined I was feeding my own childhood self, that little demon, that Devil-marked baby who had shivered in the cold. If the HOA president had known about the golden currant tree, he would have surely ordered it destroyed like the rest of the plants, so I was literally eating forbidden fruit. The tree rooted and bloomed on its wounded patch of land, and from it my daughters and I nourished our fire, our blood.

You, reading this book: You are an ark. The gods are whispering to you through the reeds. What are you carrying that's worth saving? What are you holding that must be protected and sheltered until conditions are right? Your devotion to forgotten gods and dying folkways? Your knowledge of endangered languages and stories? Your friendship with the spirits of the land you live on? Your gateways through the hedge? Witchcraft lives in your blood, crackling in the synapses of your mind and shaping itself through the pulses of your voice. Witchcraft burns inside you, and your job is to keep its embers glowing.

The children are in bed and my work for the day is finished. I creep up the stairwell to the roof, where the full moon hangs in the sky. I lay out my blanket, altar cloth, and tools. I set out my familiar's spirit house, a bull-roarer to call the spirits, and my roebuck skull.

Whipping the bull-roarer, I invite the spirits to come to me. In the north, I call to the hills where I can just see the Hollywood sign. In the east, I call to the rising planets and constellations. In the south, I call to the vast expanse of city, and in the west, I call to the ocean that lies just beyond the curve of the horizon. I call to my spirit coven, the Devil in all their guises, and the Goddess in all their forms. I raise the skull so that its antlers frame the moon. I work my spells and sing my hymns. There are neighbors in the windows of the buildings around me, but no one seems to see what I'm doing. The wind whips my hair and bats soar above me. Around me, Ceridwen's cauldron churns. Here, in the chill of the stars and the scorch of the gods, I'm free.

I am your daughter, I declare, and my blood sings and sings and sings.

---

## A Spell to Build Your Ark

Take the most important thing you've ever done.

Take the kindest thing anyone's ever said to you. Pack it in paper so that it's snug. Put in some flower petals if you want, or a handful of confetti. Don't worry, it won't spill.

There's a tree you remember from your childhood. Put that tree in your ark. Give it pride of place. Let its trunk be the mast, its canopy the sails. Make sure its roots have plenty of room to push through soil and talk to mushrooms. Make sure you include every cloud that ever brushed its branches, every nest that a mother tucked against its limbs.

Take that poem you wrote. Yes, *that poem*. Of course your ark knows about it—don't act so surprised! Look, there's already a special niche waiting for it, a drawer of lacquered wood with an herbal sachet inside. And look closer: There's also a blank piece of paper and a pen, for what purpose only you can decide.

Take the most random memory you have each day, for twelve days in a row. Assemble them like a puzzle. You may laugh in surprise at how they fit together—at their hidden seams, their subtle throughlines. Everything in your ark is connected, and everything is important. Frame it and hang it on the cabin wall.

Take the songs you could listen to a thousand times on repeat. Slot them into your ark next to each other. Do it vertically, so they don't warp.

Take the face of your beloved. Of all your beloveds. Take the best memories of your ancestors and the best words of your family. Take the face of the person who never found out you had a crush on them. Nestle all of them into your ark.

Take the time you did something right. Take the time you did something wrong, but for the right reasons. Take the times you fixed something, made something, discovered something, solved something. Take the times you brightened someone's day. Take the times you improved someone's world. Don't work too hard to seek them out. When you finally admit to yourself that you've done good in this world, they'll come to you.

O Witch, take the most important spell you've ever cast, the most important prayer you've ever said, the most important charm you've ever made, the most important song you've ever sung. Put them all in your ark.

Now lay your heart on top of it all. There, just like that. It'll all be safe, I promise. Kiss your ark, wish it luck, and cast it off.

# Acknowledgments

Books are like mushrooms: They might seem discrete on the surface, but underneath the fertile soil, they prove to be the products of countless relationships and connections.

I'm profoundly grateful to everyone at Red Wheel /Weiser who saw the potential in this book: Peter Turner and Michael Kerber, who first approached me about the possibility of turning my writings into a cohesive manuscript; the marketing team, who guided me through the daunting process of learning to advocate for my own stories; and especially my editor, Amy Lyons, who worked with me tirelessly to shape the manuscript into the best version of itself. Many, many thanks to all of you.

I'm also grateful to all the editors who published earlier versions of these chapters: Rhyd Wildermuth and Mirna Wabi-Sabi at *A Beautiful Resistance* and Ritona; Melissa Madara at *Venefica Magazine*;

Anne Newkirk Niven at *Witches & Pagans* magazine; and Vonetta Young at *The Offing*. Many thanks to Alex Wrekk at Portland Button Works (now Spiral House Shop) for carrying my homemade zine, "The Craft: A Love Letter," before it morphed into the chapter "Antler Queens."

This book wouldn't exist without the wisdom and guidance of all the teachers I've learned from over the years, as I've studied the crafts of witchcraft, writing, and other arts. Many thanks to Laurie Lovekraft, Caduceus Antonius, Griffin Ced, Seraphina Capranos, Camelia Elias, Melissa Madara, and all the other witches I've studied with over the years. Thanks to Anastasia Malliaras and Gabrielle Kaufman. Thanks to Lan Samantha Chang, Kevin Brockmeier, Ethan Canin, Marilynne Robinson, the late Jim McPherson, Joan Silber, Carolyn Ferrell, Connie Brothers, Deb West, Jan Zenisek, and all my classmates at the Iowa Writers' Workshop. I'm also grateful to all the witches I've circled with, especially Rainy Moonflower, Kirke Bonificata, Sara Fetherolf, Josh Boehm, Samantha Shay, Dominic Bodden, Amy Mackey, and Lila Amanita.

Thank you to all the witches, artists, writers, filmmakers, herbalists, and researchers working to reenchant the world. We *are* the weirdos, mister.

Obviously, I owe my family more gratitude than I can express. To Zelda and Iris: You're my miracles and my treasures, and you've transformed my life into something magical. To my sister, Lauren: Your excitement and encouragement mean so much to me. To my parents: Thank you for encouraging my growth as a writer and giving me the resources to cultivate my craft.

Finally, as always, to Tom: I wouldn't be who I am without you. You're my best friend, my staunchest cheerleader, and my partner in everything. I love you.

The following chapters appeared, in earlier forms, in the following publications:

"The Devil's Mark": *Venefica Magazine*
"Antler Queens": "The Craft: A Love Letter" (self-published zine)
"My Mother's Tarot": *Witches & Pagans*
"Morrigan, Queen of the Witches"; "Rainreturn"; "The Bee Priestess"; and "We Can All Be Arks": *Abeautifulresistance.org*
"Thy God Loki": *The Offing*

# Bibliography

Anderson, M. Kat. *Tending the Wild: Native American Knowledge and the Management of California's Natural Resources.* Berkeley: University of California Press, 2005.

Barber, Elizabeth Wayland. *Women's Work: The First 20,000 Years.* New York: Norton, 1994.

Bornstein, Carol, David Fross, and Bart O'Brien. *California Native Plants for the Garden.* Los Olivos, CA: Cachuma Press, 2005.

Boyer, Corinne. *Plants of the Devil.* Richmond Vista, CA: Three Hands Press, 2017.

Boyle, Gregory. *Barking to the Choir: The Power of Radical Kinship.* New York: Simon & Schuster, 2017.

Brown, Nancy Marie. *The Real Valkyrie: The Hidden History of Viking Warrior Women.* New York: St. Martin's Press, 2021.

Burgess, Charlie Claire. *Radical Tarot: Queer the Cards, Liberate Your Practice, and Create the Future.* Carlsbad, CA: Hay House, Inc., 2023.

Butler, Octavia E. *Dawn.* New York: Grand Central Publishing, 1987.

———. *Parable of the Talents.* New York: Grand Central Publishing, 1998.

Carlson, Rachel D. *The Honey Bee and Apian Imagery in Classical Literature.* PhD diss. University of Washington, 2015. *digital.lib.washington.edu.*

Chiang, Ted. *Exhalation: Stories.* New York: Knopf, 2019.

Clark, Rosalind. "Aspects of the Morrígan in Early Irish Literature." *Irish University Review* 17, no. 2 (1987): 223–236. *jstor.org.*

Cochrane, Robert. *The Robert Cochrane Letters: An Insight into Modern Traditional Witchcraft.* Somerset, UK: Capall Bann, 2002.

de Mattos Frisvold, Nicholaj. *Craft of the Untamed.* Oxford, UK: Mandrake, 2011.

Dore, Jessica. *Tarot for Change: Using the Cards for Self-Care, Acceptance, and Growth.* New York: Penguin, 2021.

Estés, Clarissa Pinkola. *Women Who Run with the Wolves: Myths and Stories of the Wild Woman Archetype.* New York: Ballantine Books, 1992.

Ferry, David. *Gilgamesh: A New Rendering in English Verse.* New York: Farrar, Straus and Giroux, 1992. Tablet XI.

Furlong, Monica. *Wise Child.* New York: Random House, 1987.

Garcia, Cecilia, and James D. Adams, Jr. *Healing with Medicinal Plants of the West.* La Crescenta, CA: Abedus Press, 2016.

Gladstar, Rosemary. *Medicinal Herbs: A Beginner's Guide.* North Adams, MA: Storey Publishing, 2012.

Green, Marian. *A Witch Alone.* Charlottesville, VA: Hampton Roads, 2009.

Grieve, Mrs. M. *A Modern Herbal.* New York: Dover, 1971.

Higgins, Lila, and Gregory B. Pauly. *Wild LA: Explore the Amazing Nature In and Around Los Angeles.* Portland, OR: Timber Press, 2019.

Kelly, Bernard. *Cúchulainn and the Crow Queen.* Dublin: The History Press Ireland, 2014.

Koltuv, Barbara Black. *The Book of Lilith.* Lake Worth, FL: Nicolas-Hays, Inc., 1986.

Lear, Jonathan. *Radical Hope: Ethics in the Face of Cultural Devastation.* Cambridge, MA: Harvard University Press, 2008.

Le Guin, Ursula K. *A Wizard of Earthsea.* New York: Graphia, 2012.

Madame Pamita. *Baba Yaga's Book of Witchcraft.* Woodbury, MN: Llewellyn Worldwide, 2022.

Nerenberg, Jenara. *Divergent Mind: Thriving in a World That Wasn't Designed for You.* New York: HarperOne, 2020.

Pollack, Rachel. *A Walk Through the Forest of Souls: A Tarot Journey to Spiritual Awakening.* Newburyport, MA: Weiser Books, 2002.

Starhawk. *The Fifth Sacred Thing.* New York: Random House, 1993.

Sturluson, Snorri, and Jesse L. Byock, eds. and trans. *The Prose Edda: Norse Mythology.* New York: Penguin Classics, 2006.

Timbrook, Jan. Chumash *Ethnobotany: Plant Knowledge Among the Chumash People of Southern California.* Berkeley, CA: Heyday, 2007.

Trungpa, Chogyam. *Shambhala: The Sacred Path of the Warrior.*
Boulder, CO: Shambhala, 2019.

Wilson-Rich, Noah. *The Bee: A Natural History.* Princeton, NJ:
Princeton University Press, 2018.

# About the Author

Asa West is the author of *The Witch's Kin* and *Five Principles of Green Witchcraft*, and her work has appeared in *The Offing, Joyland, Gods&Radicals*, and other publications. She holds an MFA from the Iowa Writers' Workshop and has been covering feminism and media since 2007 under the name Julia Glassman. As a journalist for The Mary Sue and other outlets, she covers everything from Marvel movies to folk horror—and, of course, all things witchy. You can find her online at *asawestauthor.com*.

# To Our Readers

Weiser Books, an imprint of Red Wheel/Weiser, publishes books across the entire spectrum of occult, esoteric, speculative, and New Age subjects. Our mission is to publish quality books that will make a difference in people's lives without advocating any one particular path or field of study. We value the integrity, originality, and depth of knowledge of our authors.

Our readers are our most important resource, and we appreciate your input, suggestions, and ideas about what you would like to see published.

Visit our website at *www.redwheelweiser.com*, where you can learn about our upcoming books and free downloads, and also find links to sign up for our newsletter and exclusive offers.

You can also contact us at info@rwwbooks.com or at

Red Wheel/Weiser, LLC
65 Parker Street, Suite 7
Newburyport, MA 01950